ASTROLOGY RULES!

Every Girl's Dream Guide to Her Stars

ASTROLOGY RULES!

Every Girl's Dream Guide to Her Stars

Debra Levere

Illustrated by Monica Gesue

VOLO

Hyperion ☾ New York

Printed in the United States of America
First Edition
1 3 5 7 9 10 8 6 4 2
ISBN 0-7868-1511-6
Library of Congress Catalog Card Number: 00–109911

Visit www.volobooks.com

For my father,
Dr. Arthur Levere,
who is playing golf in the sky.
He always told me
to stick to poetry

Thanks
to my lucky stars, especially
the two VIP Libras in my life: my
astute editor, Alessandra Balzer, who
helped me shape the book, and the
undying support of my agent,
Regula Noetzli

CONTENTS

SIGNS OF SUMMER: CANCER, LEO, AND VIRGO

THE SUMMER SPIRIT • 89

SIGNS OF WINTER: CAPRICORN, AQUARIUS, AND PISCES

INTRODUCTION

AS RECENTLY AS SIXTY YEARS AGO ASTROLOGY WAS CONSIDERED WITCHCRAFT. An acceptable indulgence for the royal family perhaps, but not for someone living on Elm Street, **Anywhere, USA.**

In those days, a girl's options were usually limited to school and marriage. Chaperone-free lives were reserved for rebellious heiresses or daring writers. The idea of a girl "finding herself" or having a career was as crazy as believing that the moon was made out of cheese.

Law, politics, and medicine were reserved for men only. Actresses were perceived as social outcasts, not gifted stars in designer threads speaking up for social reform. Female athletes were confined to *pretty* sports. Like ballet. Hockey? Soccer? Dream on! As for music? Anything but classical piano was considered unladylike. Imagine if Alanis or Madonna had been born before WW II—they'd *still* be stuck in the kitchen!

Enter rock 'n' roll. Women's Lib. Woodstock. Amelia Earhart. Tina Turner. *The Mod Squad*. Education became a necessity. College-bound females were no longer programmed for an "M.R.S." degree. Gutsy women in every imaginable field demolished barriers. Using flower power instead of aromatherapy, hippies brought astrology back into vogue. Asking "What's your sign?" became as common as asking for an e-mail address today. Soul-searching then was as hip as owning a cell phone now.

In the '90s, the school of Self-Discovery was unofficially christened The New Age. Cosmic analysis became serious business. Corporations consulted astrologers to get the edge on future financial trends. Couples ordered compatibility charts before tying the knot. Star power became woven into the fabric of daily life.

Astrology has become a powerful tool that provides a microscopic view of character and a telescopic view of the future. And this relates to me how? you might ask.

Your birth chart is full of survival tools to help you deal with life's most challenging chapter: adolescence.

Teen-aging can feel like a mystical journey one minute, an allergy the next. Moods morph hourly. **Hormones rage.** Your body becomes an alien. Tryouts, midterms, and auditions make you feel like a floppy disk. Popularity and dating dilemmas define your already wobbly self-esteem. Brain-tweaking crushes can cause a concentration meltdown, making the mere thought of homework a total joke.

Intensity rules. No one *gets* it. Daily dramas spin you out until you completely space on what you were just obsessing about a minute ago. **"Feeling fat"** freak-outs lead to the dreaded wardrobe crisis—winning the Homeroom Fashion Olympics becomes the impossible dream.

ASTROLOGY TO THE RESCUE!

Astrology is your astral antidote to life on planet Earth. Connect to the celestial 411. Get hip to your talents and trip-ups by decoding the secret language of the stars. Discover the real deal on your Sun, Moon, and Rising sign. Know how very cool it is to be born a "Cusp Kid."

Get the lowdown on compatibility. Armed with a cosmic compass and black belt in romance, navigate the road rage of relationships fending off all losers. Make this astro guide your new best friend. Your secret weapon.

WHAT'S A HOROSCOPE?

Think of your natal birth chart as a permanent homepage, linked 24/7 to the Cosmic Discovery Channel. The word "natal" means "birth" in Latin. The word "horoscope" is derived from the Greek *hōra*, "hour," and *skopos*, "watcher." *Natal horoscope* literally means **"birth hour view."**

A correct chart depends on when you were born and where. This data lets the astrologer convert earth time into **sidereal**, or star, time. Knowing star time allows the astrologer to do your chart. Like snowflakes, no two 'scopes are the same. Even twins have distinct charts: a matter of a few minutes can change everything.

Your chart's one-of-a-kind planetary pattern reveals clues to your personality and potential.

The planets constantly move around a belt-shaped circle in the sky called the **Zodiac**, which contains the twelve constellations we know as Sun signs. Your chart freezes the planets on a two-dimensional plane at the exact moment when you were born. An astrologer can look at any chart and see a **"theme,"** explain why you do what you do, and predict minor and major turning points.

Planetary motions are called transits. **Transits "trigger" points** on your natal chart daily and make things happen. Some transits are fast, fleeting, and **fun,** others are slower, long lasting, and serious. Magazines and newspaper horoscopes are based on transits in relation to your Sun sign.

For a more **accurate** forecast, always read *both* your Rising and Sun sign predictions. Additionally, if you are born on a cusp, always read the two signs you straddle.

But remember, it's all up to you. You *always* have the power of free will. Astrology is a **cosmic weather report** that helps you decide.

Will you skip class, or finish that essay? Will you hide in homeroom when he walks by, or pluck up the courage to say hello?

WHY DO WE USE THE SUN?

Viewed from Earth, the Sun cruises around the galaxy at a predictable speed, transiting into each sign on the same day every year, give or take twenty-four to forty-eight hours. The **speeds** of the other planets are very different. Example? The Moon takes two and a half days to go through a sign while Saturn takes two and a half years.

The three most powerful elements in your chart are the **Sun,** which governs *what you do*; the **Moon,** *how you feel*; and the **Ascendant,** *who you are*.

BUT WHAT'S AN ASCENDANT, ANYWAY?

Your Ascendant or Rising sign (same thing) is the sign of the Zodiac that was rising on the horizon at the second you were born. Have you ever read something about your Sun sign and thought, That's *so* not me! **Blame your Ascendant.** Your Rising sign is so powerful, people usually think you *are* that sign. Often called the "door" you open to the world, the ascendant even determines your looks. If you know when you were born or even *around* when you were born, check out your Ascendant in the table on the next page.

ASCENDANT CHART

SUN SIGNS	12AM–2AM	2AM–4AM	4AM–6AM	6AM–8AM	8AM–10AM	10AM–12PM	12PM–2PM	2PM–4PM	4PM–6PM	6PM–8PM	8PM–10PM	10PM–12AM
ARIES	capricorn	aquarius	pisces	aries	taurus	gemini	cancer	leo	virgo	libra	scorpio	sagittarius
TAURUS	aquarius	pisces	aries	taurus	gemini	cancer	leo	virgo	libra	scorpio	sagittarius	capricorn
GEMINI	pisces	aries	taurus	gemini	cancer	leo	virgo	libra	scorpio	sagittarius	capricorn	aquarius
CANCER	aries	taurus	gemini	cancer	leo	virgo	libra	scorpio	sagittarius	capricorn	aquarius	pisces
LEO	taurus	gemini	cancer	leo	virgo	libra	scorpio	sagittarius	capricorn	aquarius	pisces	aries
VIRGO	gemini	cancer	leo	virgo	libra	scorpio	sagittarius	capricorn	aquarius	pisces	aries	taurus
LIBRA	cancer	leo	virgo	libra	scorpio	sagittarius	capricorn	aquarius	pisces	aries	taurus	gemini
SCORPIO	leo	virgo	libra	scorpio	sagittarius	capricorn	aquarius	pisces	aries	taurus	gemini	cancer
SAGITTARIUS	virgo	libra	scorpio	sagittarius	capricorn	aquarius	pisces	aries	taurus	gemini	cancer	leo
CAPRICORN	libra	scorpio	sagittarius	capricorn	aquarius	pisces	aries	taurus	gemini	cancer	leo	virgo
AQUARIUS	scorpio	sagittarius	capricorn	aquarius	pisces	aries	taurus	gemini	cancer	leo	virgo	libra
PISCES	sagittarius	capricorn	aquarius	pisces	aries	taurus	gemini	cancer	leo	virgo	libra	scorpio

OKAY, NOW I KNOW MY ASCENDANT— WHAT DOES IT MEAN?

Aries Rising

UPSIDE

You *do* stuff, you don't just *say* stuff. **A born leader,** you attack life. Your mission? Just to change the world. Headstrong, the word *no* is not in your vocabulary. Energy level? Off the Richter scale. To say you're athletic is an understatement, but with team sports, you've *got to be* captain.

DOWNSIDE

Rushing around like you do, you could miss out on the subtle side of life. (Like you care!) You can be impatient with people who *just don't get it.* Your **"win at all costs"** attitude could make you blow right by potentially awesome friends and boyfriends. Face it; you leave everyone in the dust.

PERSONAL APPEARANCE

Aries rules the face, so **your looks are unforgettable.** You're a body in motion with a lean, muscular build. Regardless of actual weight, you appear strong. Mars, the Warrior Princess, rules Aries. You're bold. Bewitching.

Taurus Rising
UPSIDE

Possessions and getting "things" makes you feel safe. You have a sixth sense when it comes to **comfort, color,** and **style.** Magnetic. Loyal. You radiate depth. Your character is set early. As a child you shocked adults with your matter-of-fact wisdom. Phonies bug you. Imaginative, you're drawn to the arts. Taurus rules the throat, so you could have an amazing voice.

DOWNSIDE

Bullheaded, you can't deal with change. You'd rather stay in a bad situation because at least you know what to expect. When people don't do what you want, how you want, when you want, boy can you sulk! You redefine the word *lazy*. You are addicted to fast food and can really stuff that face. Jealousy creeps into your bloodstream in a microsecond. You're the master of putting things off till 3 A.M.

PERSONAL APPEARANCE

Venus, the symbol of physical perfection, rules Taurus. You emit an **earthy beauty.** Taurus Rising natives are rarely "model thin," so weight could be a problem, *especially in your mind.* Your thick hair has volume, body, curls, and shine.

Gemini Rising
UPSIDE

Flirty. Charming. Agile. Faster than light. **The stuff of celebrity.** Poetic. Flexible. Verbal. Intellectual. Social diva. Most subjects captivate you . . . for at least a week, maybe! Routine gives you hives. Your mind grasps ideas faster than e-mails fly. *Short-term* is your thing.

DOWNSIDE

Attention span is a problem. You can't commit because you never know if something better is coming. High-strung, hyper, and nervous. Impossible to pin down. Your sudden disinterest in things can make you seem shallow. Changing circles virtually overnight tweaks out friends who thought they knew you. Nickname? Chameleon.

PERSONAL APPEARANCE

Slender. Perpetually youthful. Typically tall. Long, straight, or ski-jump nose. Hazel, aqua, or unusually beautiful eye color. **Typical crush material** looks-wise. Flawless skin. Elegant-boned. Glamorous. Trendsetter.

Cancer Rising

UPSIDE

You're original. Proactive. Sensitive. A genius investor. **Intuition verges on ESP.** Your memory is remarkable. You're domestic and a terrific cook *when you feel like it*. Sympathetic. Connected to the past in a positive way. You know how to nurture things of emotional value.

DOWNSIDE

Your mood swings are notorious. People tiptoe around you to make sure the coast is clear. Secretive by nature, **you'd rather die than open up.** It's not that you're cheap; it's just that you're saving for that rainy day . . . like, forever. You hold grudges. Melancholy, guarded, and hypersensitive, you personalize everything.

PERSONAL APPEARANCE

Luminous complexion. Dewy eyes. Moon-shaped face. **Mysterious.** Alluring. Sexy. Tend to be short. Full-breasted. Photogenic.

Leo Rising

UPSIDE

Fearless. Peerless. Royal. Proud. A real head-turner. Dramatic. A diva in search of an audience. Beyond generous. **Loyal.** Your common sense is enviable. You can't understand why people do stupid things. A natural promoter, you always try to help your friends. In charge. Your awesome multiple talents lead to **fame, glory,** and **success.** Big-hearted, you attract great partners. The opposite of dull.

DOWNSIDE

You can come off conceited, become a drama-queen, or go into diva mode without warning. Bossy. You have to have the best. Credit-card debt could be in your future.

PERSONAL APPEARANCE

Even if you buy clothes in petites, you seem ten feet tall. Regal, poised, and dignified, **you exude importance.** You have a fabulous mane of hair, like the Lion. You have strong features—star material.

Virgo Rising

UPSIDE

An organization princess, **you plot better than the FBI.** An earth sign symbolizing the harvest, you reap rewards in your garden of ideas. A brilliant analyst, you can assess a situation just by walking in the door. A whiz with detail and texture, design could be your destiny. An astute critic, you're a natural editor and writer.

DOWNSIDE

Your need to be perfect at all times thrusts you into a **personal pressure cooker.** Your instinct to automatically dissect things makes you see what's wrong instead of what's right. People can never measure up. Food-finicky, your digestive system is very delicate.

PERSONAL APPEARANCE

A broad forehead, fine nose, small chin. Very sophisticated. You're always perfecting your look. You adore earthy tones and won't wear anything that draws attention. On the slender side. Fashion is your passion.

Libra Rising

UPSIDE

Lucky you! Libra rising gifts you with grace, magnetism, and supernatural charm. You're the type to tumble out of bed on a bad hair day and *still* look good. A "we" person, you're **social** and **dynamic.** You bring harmony and balance into the world. You discover yourself through relationships.

DOWNSIDE

You see yourself through other people's reactions. If someone looks at you the wrong way, you bungee jump into the **emotional Bermuda Triangle.**

PERSONAL APPEARANCE

This ascendant is the **Zodiac's Big Enchilada** in the Looks Department. Most supermodels, male and female, have Libra Rising. Perfectly proportioned, this indicates God or Goddess stature.

Scorpio Rising

UPSIDE

Spiritually powerful, you pursue your dreams with intensity. You never, ever quit. You'll do something till your knees are bloody. An "old soul," inner vision guides you. You have "instant karma" and constantly reinvent yourself. The opposite of shallow, you're the **Terminator of the Zodiac.**

DOWNSIDE

Your probing style can intimidate. When you get mad, you go in so deep; nobody can reach you. It's like the **committee between your ears** is at an impasse. If things don't go your way, you spin out. When things look grim, you could actually believe things are never going to change.

PERSONAL APPEARANCE

There is **nothing vague** about your looks. Piercing eyes and strong features. You may battle your weight and have drastic changes in your physical appearance throughout your life. Sometimes you feel like your body is in one state and your head is in another. You "develop" early. Dad worries . . . a lot!

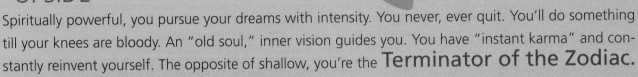

Sagittarius Rising

UPSIDE

The most spiritual sign, your "search" never ends because there's always more, more, more! You were born with a **cosmic fortune cookie** in your mouth. You're carefree, spontaneous, athletic. Travel and higher education are your fate, whether through career or relationships. You dare to explore things nobody else will. *Nothing* scares you.

DOWNSIDE

You exaggerate. Your "stories" are so real, you actually believe them. You're so blunt, people think you're rude. The human flash—no one can get close. You have a zillion friends but don't spend too much time with any one person. You can talk someone's ear off and never tell them a thing. Your competitive streak is so high, it's hard for you to be a team player.

PERSONAL APPEARANCE

Jupiter rules Sag, which rules the thighs. You have **great legs,** muscular and swift. Jupiter knows no boundaries, and that goes for food, too. A walking example of mind over matter, you can purposely gain or lose weight fast when you set your mind to it.

Capricorn Rising

UPSIDE

Patient, stealthy, and cautious, you're able to wait out any situation until the timing is right. You have **your eye on the gold,** no matter how long it takes. You may know your purpose in life from the age of three. You're able to impose order on chaos and structure things. Defeat only elevates your resolve to win.

DOWNSIDE

Miss Doom and Gloom, you fear the worst. You can believe that things will only get worse. **You worry a lot,** but hide it because you can't afford to look bad. You can be a real loner and believe the world is against you. Call a friend—they'll tell you it's not!

PERSONAL APPEARANCE

Capricorn's symbol is the sea-goat: a mountain goat with the tail of a mermaid. Meaning? Unconscious dreams (mermaid) motivate you to climb the mountain of accomplishment (mountain goat). This doesn't mean you resemble an actual goat! It means you have the more flattering aspects of this nimble creature. You are **compact, agile,** on the **petite** side, with defined cheekbones. Since Cap rules the knees, your legs are likely to be your best feature.

Aquarius Rising

UPSIDE

An **absolute original.** A visionary. Ahead of your time. Electric. Genius. An Internet wizard. You're so smart, you make teachers look dumb. You start revolutions. You're on a mission to change the world. You're the kind of person to join the Peace Corps.

DOWNSIDE

You're such an eccentric; you enjoy shocking the world for the sake of being "different." Being **"on a mission,"** you can spend your entire life with virtual strangers. Getting close to people could terrify you.

PERSONAL APPEARANCE

With your wild eyes, people sense you're telepathic. Long-limbed and wiry, your movements are electric and unpredictable. You have **movie-star looks.** Your remote demeanor makes other people desire you more.

Pisces Rising

UPSIDE

Your psychic gifts are profound. You adapt to different environments quickly. **Creativity and artistic vibrations** captivate you. Music, songs, and lyrics literally pour out of you. You are driven to help the less fortunate.

DOWNSIDE

You can't distinguish between fantasy and reality. Mood swings hijack your head. **You seek oblivion.** You're absentminded. You can be manipulative because you know just how to hook people into your schemes.

PERSONAL APPEARANCE

Your eyes are dreamy. It's like you see right through people into their real intentions. A glamour girl, you are **extremely feminine.** As a Water sign, you have a tendency to gain more water weight than other Rising signs.

THE HOUSES: AN OVERVIEW

Envision a circle divided in twelve sections, like a pie. These twelve "sectors" are called houses. The first house is located underneath the left side of the horizon line and continues around the circle in a counterclockwise motion. Each "house" represents an area of life experience. Houses containing planets pinpoint areas where you channel the most energy.

In order to analyze your horoscope even further, astrologers break down the horoscope by dividing it in two with a "Horizon Line," which separates the circle into the Lower and Upper Hemispheres. Each hemisphere has a meaning.

Houses one through six comprise the Lower Hemisphere, the **"Me" houses** that deal with your inner life. Houses seven through twelve comprise the Upper Hemisphere, the **"We" houses,** which explain how you relate to the outside world.

Astrologers also bestow meaning to the four angles in the horoscope. These angles or points are located on the east (right), south (bottom), west (left), and north (top).

The Ascendant is located on the first-house "cusp"—the east angle. The Ascendant explains your personality.

The Descendant is located on the seventh-house cusp, opposite the Ascendant, the west angle. This determines the type of relationships and partner you're likely to attract.

The south point of the chart is called the Nadir and is located on the fourth-house cusp. The Nadir symbolizes your innermost self. It is also called the "processing point" because it shows how you process outside influences. The Mid-heaven is located on the tenth-house cusp at the chart's north point. It describes your public profile, popularity, reputation, and career.

MORE ABOUT THE HOUSES

1ST HOUSE
Aries—Spring, The Vernal Equinox

MEANING: Beginnings. The "I." Physical appearance. Self-image. Personality. Attitude. Outlook. Immediate environment.

2ND HOUSE
Taurus

MEANING: Values. Property. Possessions. Money. Earning potential. Personal resources. Innate talents. Drive for material security.

3RD HOUSE
Gemini

MEANING: Siblings. Early education. Consciousness. Short trips. Neighbors, relatives, and neighborhood. Communication. Writing and speaking. Networking.

4TH HOUSE
Cancer—The Summer Solstice

MEANING: Home. Cooking. Family. Solitude. The mother figure. Endings. Foundations. Nurturing. Yin energy. Emotion. Memory.

5TH HOUSE
Leo

MEANING: Romance. Fun. Risks. Self-expression. Theater. Acting. Creation. Love affairs. Dating. Sports. Children. Competition. Entertainment. Parties.

6TH HOUSE
Virgo

MEANING: Health. Health issues. Habits. Pets. Service. Work. Jobs. Employees. Diet. The healing arts. Fashion design. Fabric. Texture. Precision.

7TH HOUSE
Libra—The Autumnal Equinox

MEANING: "We," "Others." Major relationships. Contracts. Marriage. Partnerships. Enemies you know about. Competitors. Negotiations. Commitment.

8TH HOUSE
Scorpio

MEANING: Other people's resources, chiefly money and property. Estate issues. Sexual relationships. Sexuality. Death. Taxes. Inheritance. Regeneration. Personal transformation. Karma.

9TH HOUSE
Sagittarius

MEANING: The "quest." Advanced schooling. Publishing. Award. Benefits. Scholarship. Philosophy. Foreign travel. Languages. Spirituality. Religion. The Law. In-laws.

10TH HOUSE
Capricorn—The Winter Solstice

MEANING: Status. Ambition. Career. Reputation. Government. Mentors and father figures. Fame. Celebrity. Accomplishment.

11TH HOUSE
Aquarius

MEANING: Collaborations. Groups. Ideals. Vision. Hopes. Dreams. Friendships. Social connections. Charity. Clubs. Teams. Entrepreneurial spirit. Genius.

12TH HOUSE
Pisces

MEANING: Dreams. Illusion. Celluloid. Fantasy. Psychic power. Escapism. Inspiration. Prophecy. Self-sabotage. Subconscious. Sacrifice. Prayer. Secret relationships. Confined spaces.

TO EVERYTHING, THERE IS A SEASON...

Astrology reflects the seasons. The astrological year doesn't begin on January 1; it starts on the first day of spring and ends on the last day of winter.

Being born within a specific season gives you that season's flavor. Using this sensible seasonal strategy blows mass-market compatibility clichés out the window and explains why "nontraditional" astrological couplings can succeed.

Love matches like Aries–Taurus (Spring), Leo–Virgo (Summer), Libra–Scorpio (Autumn), and Aquarius–Pisces (Winter) make stellar sense. Same-season signs "get" each other. The reason? The close orbits of the personal planets—Moon, Mercury, Venus, and Mars.

IT'S ELEMENTAL

Earth, Fire, Water, and Air are the four astrological elements. Signs of the same element are positioned 120 degrees apart, creating a pleasant aspect called a **"trine."**

This trine aspect explains why your best love links are usually signs with the same element.

A QUALITY MATTER

In addition to elements, every sign has a "quality." Either Cardinal, Fixed, or Mutable, each quality has a specific job in defining that season.

The job of the **Cardinal** signs is to formally bring a season's energy into being.

Fixed signs always follow Cardinals. Their job is to stabilize a season's energy. They "fixate" things.

Mutable signs are the third and last signs, of each season. Their function is to convert the energy of one season into the next.

Look at it like this: The pioneering Cardinal sign of Aries goes out in the wild and discovers untouched, fertile land.

Then comes Fixed Taurus, who sees the land's worth and decides to build a house and claim the territory.

Now that Aries has gone off to his or her next **adventure,** Taurus plunks down and goes to work. Realistic and money-minded, she budgets for essentials, like the architects and contractors.

Enter media-and-communications whiz kid, Mutable Gemini, who wires the house for sound. The Twin installs the phone, rigs the cable and satellite dish, sets up the computer workstation, and e-mails invitations to the house-warming party.

PLANETARY RULES

Just as psychology gives us insight into why we do what we do, astrology reveals who we are. Each planet stands for a part of our **mind** or **personality.** Your horoscope is a personalized road map to your life, revealing behavior patterns, strengths, and weaknesses.

THE PERSONAL PLANETS

Mercury, Venus, and Mars are called "personal planets" and account for how you **think, talk, dress,** love, work, create, and function on a day-to-day basis in the world. They're what help you develop relationships, style, and personality.

Except for the Moon, personal planets can never be located more than two houses before or after your Sun sign.

Since the **slower,** outer planets (Jupiter, Saturn, Uranus, Neptune, and Pluto) stay in signs much longer, your peers will usually have these planets in the same sign as you. The effect of these planets is considered **"generational"** because they influence how an entire peer group behaves, thinks, and feels.

THE MOON

A girl's best friend or worst enemy, the Moon influences everything from moods to menstrual cycles. The emotional, vulnerable, and secretive Moon *always* defines personal or intimate relationships. Every new Moon is always followed by the full Moon in exactly two weeks. Cosmic clockwork in action!

Centuries ago, society was composed of hunter-gatherers, who depended on game and foraging to survive. They studied planetary movements to figure out the timing of things. They lived by the **waxing** and **waning** phases of the Moon. The Moon waxes as it goes from new to full, and wanes when it goes from full to new.

Waxing cycles are when to initiate things, start relationships, and put ideas out there. It's a time of new growth.

The waning phase is when to pull back, review, and finish old business . . . like cleaning out your closet—that is, if you can find it!

Stressed Situation

Have you ever met a totally cool girl or guy, but even though there was nothing "off" about them on the surface and your friends actually liked them, they just got on your nerves!? Why?

ASTRO ANSWER: Clash of your Moon sign with his or her Sun sign.

Blessed Situation

So you met a gorgeous guy. Maybe he's a little quirky, but you totally understand him despite the fact that everyone else doesn't. Explanation?

ASTRO ANSWER: It's your Moon sign talking. When your Moon is in harmonious aspect to his Sun, romantic Venus, sexy Mars or, chatty Mercury, the Milky Way's the limit to *this* bond.

Lunar Logic

MERCURY

The Cosmic Messenger, Mercury rules language, communications, early education, the conscious mind, writing ability, and the intellect. The sign that Mercury was in when you were born determines whether you're a shy girl into long nights buried in books, or a party girl with exceptional flirting skills.

VENUS AND MARS

Venus and Mars are two potent sides of the same coin. Venus pulls and magnetizes; Mars pushes and asserts. Venus is the Goddess of Love; Mars is the God of War. Mars is about action, competition, and athleticism. Venus is about harmony, beauty, and grace.

Astro romance tip:
A guy's Venus placement tells about the girl he dreams of; a girl's Mars placement tells you what she looks for in a guy.

SIGNS OF SPRING

ARIES, TAURUS, AND GEMINI

THE SPRING SPIRIT

SPRINGTIME IS WHEN WINTER COLD DOES A SLOW FADE. Snow melts. Emotions come out of a deep freeze. Hibernation ends. **Your spirit is set free.** Expectations multiply. Infatuations bloom. You awake from winter's slumber. Daylight evens out and overtakes the night. More daylight means more playtime.

Your team and teen spirit returns with a vengeance. You increase your activities. You're in no mood to slack off. New social situations present themselves daily. Your popularity factor climbs. You're radiant. Decisive about the future.

Inspiration comes through like lightning bolts. You develop a "spring-cleaning" frame of mind.

You release things that no longer feel right. You examine your position on the food chain and review successes and setbacks. You obsess about what you think you should have and where you think you should be. You get hip to yourself.

Spring signs are barrier-breakers. Pioneers. Doers. Believers in magic and fate. Spring signs make things happen. You epitomize the miracle of new life. The talent to create is built into your DNA.

Aries, Taurus, and Gemini are the signs of the Creators.

You create your own future by taking over. Spring fever is a permanent mind-set. A wild child, you stake out new territories. But your notoriously short attention span can prevent you from seeing things through to completion.

Astro Advice

Surround yourself with responsible people. People born later in the astrological year tend to follow through. Boost your chances for success by consciously seeking them out.

Cosmic Challenge

Shoot for the good kind of attention. Count to ten before giving in to an impulse. Try to think things through. Check your motives.

Like a toddler who gets into **just about everything**, you Spring signs are perpetually curious. Your essence is naïve. Your inquisitive nature gets you into all kinds of things. And like a child, you can be naughty.

You are a prankster, prone to episodes of immaturity. A rebel with *or* without a cause. You always have an excuse. You get away with murder.

Then there is your legendary **"I want what I want when I want it"** act. You stomp your feet until you get what you want. People give in. You put yourself first. The opposite of shy, you can never get enough attention. Your **can't ignore charisma** makes you a born leader. No one can stay mad at you.

As Creators of the Zodiac, you need to be in charge. Your leadership abilities are obvious from childhood. You're always the one who people try to imitate. Even if you go through an awkward phase, just wait! During those painful years, you're hatching a success strategy that will blow everybody else out of the water.

You can't stand being second best. You never hesitate to make your opinions known. Propelled by the urge to win, you need to be in front, be the best, the fastest, smartest, or the prettiest. You set the pace; other people follow. You set the tone; other people comply. Who can fight Mother Nature?

ARIES

MARCH 21 – APRIL 20

RULING PLANET:
mars

SYMBOL:
the ram

SEASON:
spring

QUALITY:
cardinal

ELEMENT:
fire

COLORS:
power red, champagne yellow, and salmon

POWER STONES:
diamond, ruby, and sapphire

BODY:
head and face

FLOWERS:
geranium, red camellia, and gladiolus

CITIES:
naples, palo alto, florence, krakow, and birmingham (u.k.)

COUNTRIES:
england, france, and germany

VIBRATION:
irresistible, impatient, irreverent, and invincible

ZODIAC HOUSE:
first

KEY WORDS:
i discover who i am by taking action.

WHAT AM I LIKE?

ARIES EQUALS PURE ENERGY.

Symbolically, Aries represents the Big Bang that began our Universe. Aries starts the astrological year with the first day of Spring, which is called the "Vernal Equinox." The Vernal Equinox separates Winter from Spring.

Aries is first. Aries leads. You are the Warrior Princess. **Think Xena!** You speak your mind and will not take no for an answer. You are the opposite of shy. The world exists for you to conquer. You are **fearless** and **confident**. You generate excitement just by showing up. Enthusiasm pours from your every pore. **You are a Cardinal Fire sign.** Cardinal signs start seasons.

Fire signs are committed to living a life of action instead of words. Of course, you're verbal, but you rarely live in a dream world. If you talk about something, chances are you'll wind up doing it.

You're so fast, few signs can keep up. Your **"me, me, more about me"** attitude can put people off, but you don't really care.

You are intolerant and impatient. When somebody is incapable of seeing the obvious, you get annoyed. You can destroy somebody's confidence with a look. You can be **arrogant. Conceited. Bigheaded.**

If you're popular, you're capable of deciding who's cool.

Your competitive streak is significant. Things usually come easy. If there's an obstacle, you'll overcome it. The phrase "I can't" is not in your vocabulary.

You would rather pretend you know what you are

doing than admit you need help.

Challenge **excites** you. You will go after something for the sake of winning, whether or not you really want it. Like with guys. You will go after the hardest one just to prove to yourself you can win him over. But once you get him and find out what he is really like, you lose interest.

With sports, you rule. You live for physical activity. Since you are the "me first" sign, you like solo sports. With team sports, you have to be captain. **You hate to lose.**

Friendship is important because you need allies. You see the world in terms of teammates and competitors.

You only make the effort if they can assist you in some way.

It's not that you don't need love, support, or emotional contact, but frankly, you think all that stuff is **overrated**.

You're great at maintaining relationships. You keep friends for years, because if they met your standards in the first place, you know they'll continue to succeed.

The touchy-feely part of friendship makes you **restless.** You cannot stay on the phone listening to the same story dissected, analyzed, and interpreted. You like to get straight to the point. Anything else is a waste of time.

With relationships, your competitive mode can boomerang. Your idea of **"working out"** a problem is talking the other person into a coma.

MY ASTRO HOUSE

ARIES RULES THE FIRST HOUSE OF THE ZODIAC.

This is the house of the personality, physical appearance, and immediate environment. More than most, your looks determine your character, your identity. You always make an impression. People remember you, even if they saw you in a crowd.

Competitive, **assertive**, and **aggressive,** Mars rules the first house. You are bold. You only learn by doing. You are so quick, you don't repeat mistakes too frequently.

You have to win. You actually enjoy conflict. Break up to make up. You live for the thrill of the battle. You feel driven to make an impact on your immediate environment. **You run your empire.** You create your own rules. But you love to change the system even more.

Aries rules the head and face. You may have hit your head, scarred your face, or have some distinctive facial marking.

Astro Insight

Appearances are important to you. First impressions stick. It is difficult for you to give anybody a second chance if they don't get your attention right away.

Aries

HOW DOES MY PLANETARY RULER, MARS, AFFECT ME?

IN THE CHINESE SCHOOL OF THOUGHT, energy is divided into yin, feminine spirit, and yang, masculine fuel. Mars is pure yang. It is the planet of competition, desire, and action. Mars is the planetary partner of Venus. **Mars is the ancient god of war.** With you female Rams, Mars expresses itself through your personality as the Warrior Princess. Any woman through the course of history who fought a battle illustrates the positive side of Mars.

Don't believe for a minute that having Mars as your ruler makes you less attractive, less feminine, or less of a girl.

Mars is what makes you dynamic and confident. You have enormous willpower, ambition, and courage. You don't just talk about stuff, you do stuff. Aries embodies that age-old truth: actions speak louder than words.

Mars is volatile and emotional. Driven by your feelings, you have great enthusiasm for what you like, but are equally passionate about things you don't. **Being vague is not your style.**

Mars gives you psychic radar. It's like survival sensors were installed at birth. You can tell when a pursuit of a crush or school project becomes unrealistic. You can shift gears on command. You use time to your advantage.

Mars is considered the **planetary "bad boy,"** second only to Pluto, which rules Scorpio. Before Pluto's discovery in the 1930s, Mars ruled both Aries and Scorpio.

Mars is muscle and desire. You cannot deal with failure. You bury feelings that resurface in the form of accidents and arguments. If you allow frustrations to build, things could become unmanageable.

MY FAMILY

THE CURIOUS THING ABOUT YOUR WARRIOR PRINCESS PERSONALITY is your need to feel rooted. Your sense of family runs deep.

Despite your visible and active role in the outside world, you never feel right if things are funky at home. The reason? **Nurturing Cancer** is on the fourth-house cusp in your solar chart. You derive soul satisfaction from knowing you have a place at home that is totally off-limits to everyone else. It could be your bedroom, bathroom, or a tree house.

Siblings are superimportant to you. If your brother or sister leaves you out of things, it hurts. A sibling can affect you like nobody else. They have that kind of power. On the other side, if you do get along with a brother or a sister, it's for life. No other relationship comes close.

With your parents, the key word is nurture. There can either be an over-abundance of this, where you could feel **overprotected, claustro-phobic, and suffocated.** Or, a parent could be remote, disinterested, and withhold the emotional support you so seriously need.

It is an astrological fact that family systems share similar planetary patterns. This explains why you feel so connected to your family. The powerful pull of your family stabilizes you.

WHAT SHOULD I BE DOING

THE ONE TRUE THING ABOUT ARIES is that whatever you do brings success and puts you **ahead of the pack.** With serious things like grades, long-term goals, and deciding what will bring you satisfaction, your impatience could backfire. When things don't happen fast enough for you, you go ballistic.

You feel suffocated when you're tied down to one thing too quickly. Your first instinct is to rebel. Pressures from authority figures turn you into a **stress ball** in a microsecond.

CAREER

WHEN IT COMES TO CAREER OPTIONS, you

will only be happy in a **fast-paced** field. You will wither and die in a dead-end, blah gig. You need action. You seek adrenaline-intensive situations. You have to be in the center of things.

Wall Street is your ultimate fix when it comes to **excitement.** Making money can feel like an aphrodisiac. Ask anyone who plays or works in the stock market.

Think news reporter or on-camera personality. News never stops; it's a **24/7** thing. You thrive on deadlines. This lifestyle fulfills your need to "get there first," and be on the front lines.

WITH MY LIFE?

Forces of nature, like that dangerous new love interest, may tempt you to stray from your plans. **Risky** things entice you. Or, you will suddenly be struck with an idea and announce that you know what you want to do for the rest of your life and that is that!

The **up-to-the-minute** fashion world is your element. Model, booker, make-up magician, photographer, designer, or hair stylist, this world gives you that daily dose of excitement that makes you feel alive.

Many star sibs listed at the end of your Sun sign chapter are prominent actors, performers, and singers. A number of notable Aries also toil **behind the camera:** writers, choreographers, directors, and agents. The roller-coaster ride associated with living in this world could lure you in. The movie and TV business is notoriously **competitive** and could be right up your alley.

Being a lawyer could bore you after practicing a while, but having this degree can land you a **high-profile** job in a more exciting field. Or you'll love the litigation side where you take center stage in the courtroom, fighting battles every day.

Mars rules surgery, steel, and knives. Medicine could be an appealing lifestyle where you work daily in the theater of life and death.

If you get married young, you need to continue to create personal challenges for yourself. It's never too late to go back to school. You **CAN** have it all.

Act 1 Scene 1

STARS TIPS ON FASHION,

YOU RAMS USUALLY LEAD THE POPULARITY PACK. This puts you in the pressure cooker. People are watching. You always have to be on top of the next best thing.

Since Aries rules the face, **zit-intensive** times are almost unavoidable. If you have acne and your family can afford a good dermatologist, go! Appropriate medication speeds elimination of this epidermal enemy. Do not be afraid to ask questions. If your family cannot afford a doctor, research on the Internet. Educate yourself from Web sights, chat rooms, and medical articles directly related to your skin issues.

With makeup, find a routine that takes less than ten minutes. You're **always on the go,** athletic, and cannot be bothered with a tedious makeup regime.

Clueless? Go to the mall with a friend. Pretend you're doing a research for a fact-finding mission. Hit every cosmetic station, and ask the rep questions. Find out as much as possible about your skin and what colors you should use.

Most drugstores carry less expensive brands of makeup that are made of exactly the same stuff without the cost of advertising and personnel. Use facial exfoliants, clay masques, and *never, ever* crash with your makeup on. **Never!**

Always have a supply of hair accessories. Experiment. Braids, ponytails, dreads. Your sign rules the face. Don't hide it. Find a cut that accentuates and frames your face. Have fun with colors or easy-to-wash-out streaks.

You're a shower person; baths take too long. Scrub dead cells away with a loofa and moisturizing shower gels. Use nail polish that dries in **less than sixty seconds.** Find skin and body products that multitask for you.

Pick clothes out before you go to bed, so you avoid a morning wardrobe crisis. How many times has that perfect outfit you were planning on gotten lost in the Bermuda Triangle called your closet?

Mars is the red planet. But why confine yourself? Your personality is so strong that adding red to the equation is redundant. Muted colors like lilac, pistachio, heather, soft grays, and deeper tones like mango, coral, and boysenberry can work really well.

HEALTH, AND BEAUTY

When it comes to oils, eau de toilette, and perfume, overpowering is never a good idea. Hit the perfume counters and ask for samples. Body chemistry never lies. Less is more. **Think fresh.**

Since Aries rules the head, you could be more susceptible to headaches than the other signs. Test your vision. Limit your computer time. The ultraviolet rays from your PC or laptop when you cram or surf could cause damage. **Get plenty of rest.** Your stamina seems unlimited. But, you're the poster girl of burning the candle at both ends.

CUSP KIDZ

PISCES-ARIES: MARCH 18-22

This cusp combines the Zodiac's most spiritual and psychic sign with the most dynamic and vibrant sign. **This is the Cusp of Invincibility.**

You see through people and into their true motives, yet have the ability to do something about it. **You know things.** Your Pisces side softens the explosive Aries side. You blend action with emotion.

You are tapped into the realm of the spirit. Your impetuous Aries personality puts these intuitions to practical use.

ARIES-TAURUS: APRIL 18-22

The great thing about this cusp is that you plan your actions. Performance is tempered with consistency. **This is the Cusp of Strategy.** You have the ability to come up with new ideas and the patience to see them through. When your temper flares, you can actually count to ten. You know a tantrum will burn bridges.

The other benefit of being on this cusp is **purely cosmetic.** Your Aries charisma is enhanced by Taurus sensuality. You love the good life and the beautiful people who populate this zone.

You focus on money early in life. You know how to **make it, save it,** and, certainly, **spend it.**

COSMIC LOVE MATCHES

ARIES–ARIES
HOT, HOT, HOT!!!

More explosive than an atomic bomb. This linkup is never dull. Can you handle the heat? You're used to getting your way, but you're subtler than he is. When tempers flare, it can become a lose-lose situation. Your egos are so strong. **You both have to win.**

Do you have the patience and willingness to talk things through when they are going downhill? This combo can teach you the art of compromise. Otherwise, you won't both-er doing the work. In a temporary attraction, everyday dramas get very old, very fast. When you're through

with somebody, that's that. You're done. Since he'll do the exact same thing to you, you may recoil from getting a taste of your own medicine.

Chances are you'll end up as cautious allies. You know it would be a bad idea to be enemies; you are both too powerful. You both need to be in control, **be the star,** and look good at all times. There is not enough room in a rela-tionship for two of you. Romance is not a com-petitive sport, but with you two, you will figure out a way to keep score!

ARIES–TAURUS
SUCH A PRETTY COUPLE!

If you can deal with his **slow,** deliberate, and **thoughtful** movements, you will realize you have more in common besides a physical attraction.

Your shared spring status gives you both verve and passion. You understand each other. You both possess enough energy to go after what you want. He has the same laser focus as you, but he is **strategic,** where you are more **impulsive.** He matches your irresistible charm with his magnetic personality.

The Bull takes his time, tries things on for size, and sees how things feel. In your haste, you may have already predicted it is over, or that he is not interested, when really

ARIES–GEMINI
NEVER A DULL MOMENT

He could leave you breathless. Vitamins and power bars are strongly advised if you intend to keep up with the **Quicksilver Twin.**

Besides the fact that you are never sure which twin you are talking to, Geminis tend to be the Zodiac's most drool-worthy **crush** candidates. You never really know what they're up to, what they're thinking, or if they're playing you. Mischief is his middle name.

If anybody can handle his nonstop antics, it's you. They **intrigue, intoxicate,** and **interfere.** They get in your face. A Gemini is a challenge, probably more than you bargained for.

The Twin is adept at the art of **flirtation.** To make things harder, he's a flighty, flaky **Air sign.** His flirtation formula? The more you demand, the more he eludes your grasp. Catching a Gemini is more challenging than catching a butterfly.

Keep up your **mystique.** Let him just try to catch you—it's the only way.

Some Geminis have that annoying roving eye that kicks in when you're out on a date. If he is on the brainy side, count your blessings! Even if he is delectable, he might be oblivious to the fact that he's good-looking.

You bring each other luck and opportunity. You can be friends and romantic at the same time.
Best bet?
Be his friend first. It lasts longer.

Astro Alert

Bottom line, if he's like most Geminis, he'll get distracted or bored sooner than later. Know this has nothing to do with you even though it feels like it. In most cases, an infatuation with the Twin is fun but fleeting. He can be a real heartbreaker.

he just has not yet made up his mind.

Slow down if you think he's worth it.

Taurus never rushes. And they have absolute confidence in getting their way. Never underestimate them. They think things through. They'll have fifteen different strategies of how to play it and you.

Result? Total Flattery or Scary Stalker Material.

Astro Insight

A Bull is persuasive and can be heavy-handed. You may find this a little scary if you're not prepared or ready to go the distance.

Aries

ARIES–CANCER WEAK IN THE KNEES

Here's the first of three Cardinal-to-Cardinal couplings. Most 'scopes say: Beware! **Heartbreak Highway!** But if there's an attraction, and there probably is, you're both so clever and result-oriented that you'll make it work even if it kills you.

You're pure fire—impulsive, and brash. He's the deep end of the ocean: unfathomable, sensitive, subtle, and secretive.

Ruled by the Moon, his moods are constantly going through phases. He seeks security at all costs and avoids danger and unsafe places. You may present too great a risk of rejection, so he'll approach you with caution.

Your attraction stems from the fact that you both like to initiate things. The difference with how you initiate things is that you're direct, while he moves like a stealth bomber.

Your feelings don't get easily hurt and you don't really hold grudges. If something bugs you, you deal with it right away. With him, you hurt his feelings without even knowing what you did. He'll nurse his wounds, build a resentment, and wonder why you can't read his mind.

If you like him, truly, madly, and deeply, you must remember he's supersensitive. You may frequently have to lure him out of his crabby shell. At the first sign of danger, he'll retreat. The crab creeps backward.

ARIES–VIRGO
THE X-FILES

This combo comes under the category that fact is stranger than fiction. A Virgo tests every fiber of your being. You're on different wavelengths. No matter how hard you try, you can never figure him out.

He's too busy **analyzing** and dissecting himself, his life, and especially you. This includes an analysis of why you're together. Virgo overthinks.

Virgo is **Mr. Perfection.** He could be your personal trainer. Your tennis coach. Your diet **guru,** chiropractor, acupuncturist, or that adorable kid in the homeopathy and vitamin section at your local health-food store.

He's that guy on the track, so perfect-looking, he gives you goose bumps and the motivation to do a couple of laps yourself.

He plays by the rules. He's fascinated with what makes people tick. You could become

ARIES–LEO
A COSMIC CLASSIC

This Fire-to-Fire love link is usually a classic matchup destined for stardom. Or, if your **Fire-to-Fire** energies are too explosive, it could blow up in your face.

The one reason this combo could backfire results from the difference between your Cardinal and his Fixed quality. Your "let's go!" characteristic could clash with Leo's inflexibility.

Things roll off your back faster for you than for a Leo. And his pride! He's got **ego to burn.** He cannot afford to look bad. Nor can he tell you when his feelings get hurt. How does he handle this relationship-breaker? He doesn't.

He will act out, keep you in the dark about what you did to irritate him in the first place. But when things reach critical mass, he'll confront, combat, and act righteous. Such a serious communication meltdown may be irreparable.

But when he's into you, it's **bliss.** Generous to a fault, he'll lavish you with praise, attention, presents, and plenty of fun.

He adores showing you off in public. His middle name is **Party Central.**

Leos like to know what to expect. More than most signs, they like going out with one girl at a time. They rarely play mind games. They are faithful and loyal. It's what the "evolved Leo" is all about.

Be prepared to be spoiled rotten. He'll shower you with affection and material things that show you just how much you mean to him. The Lion is very demonstrative. He does things in a big way.

his "project" without realizing it.

Drawbacks?

He loves to isolate. If he's hard on himself, he'll be harder on you. Do you need this? He's fussy when it comes to your "look" and will turn off if you don't change right away or don't agree.

Do you need another critical parent? Only you can tell if he is giving **constructive** criticism because he wants to bring out your best.

Astro Insight

He's the guy your parents have been praying you would bring home. A Virgo knows manners and how to dress. He could give you a few tips in the wardrobe department. And he can do this without making you defensive.

ARIES–LIBRA
BLISS UNLIMITED

Your solar opposite, Mr. Charm balances you out, teaches you compassion, and calms you down. He shows you how to see all sides of a situation. Once you dive into this blissful bond, you'll learn **patience.**

You're Fire. He's Air. Wind increases a fire's intensity. You're both Cardinal signs who have the need to define yourselves through **action.**

The Libra personality is like a sponge. You're the Me sign; he's the We sign. He absorbs your vibe. Your decisive ways can help walk him through small and big things.

If you see he's agonizing over something, **talk to him.** He'll be more open than you think.

A Libra could be the best thing that has ever happened to you. He **balances** you out. He can make you look at what you are doing without making you feel like a loser. He can make you see what you're doing, before you do it.

Your yang-intensive **power planet** Mars rules you, Aries, while seductive, magnetic, and yin-intensive Venus rules Libra. This makes for a very romantic scenario.

Astro Alert

Far from being Mr. Balance, Mr. Libra seesaws. He weighs the pros and cons of things. He's indecisive. Even after he makes a decision, he can still question his choice for a very, very long time.

Astro Insight

Libras are celestially programmed to bond. He digs the relationship thing and is committed to making it work.

ARIES–SCORPIO
MANIC, TITANIC, AND TOTALLY INTENSE

As previously explained, both you and Scorpio were thought to be ruled by Mars before Pluto was discovered.

Pluto transcends the power of the Warrior Prince or Princess. Pluto deals with transformation, regeneration, and all things sexual. There

ARIES–SAGITTARIUS
SINCERELY YOURS

This is a very harmonious coupling since you're both Fire. It could be **love at first sight.** Instant chemistry. Your value systems could clash, though. He's noncommittal. You're direct. But you both create opportunities through the **sheer force** of your personalities. Wanderlust possesses him. An Archer is a *luck magnet.* Sometimes even he doesn't even know what he's looking for. You both want answers. Your relationship is based on movement and adventure. Athletics and exploration. Whether this combo lasts a semester or longer, he will expand your outlook and make you more open-minded and accepting.

is nothing shallow about this bond. You're both passionate and tend to **push the envelope.** You both live on the edge.

Your fiery Spring personality could clash with the deep, murky emotional waters of a Scorpio male.

A Scorpio is **flat-out sexy** and secretive. You're playing hardball.

If his intensity is too much, you may have to call it quits, but he doesn't give up too easily. If you're the one stuck on him, you've met your match. Once he knows you like him, he'll make you work for it.

This relationship could open you up in miraculous ways. You will discover things about your emotional makeup you never knew were there. The Scorpio factor could **change your life.**

ARIES–CAPRICORN
UNDER CONSTRUCTION

If there is one Mystery Man of the Zodiac, he's it. Capricorns appear **rock hard** and **self-sufficient.** Loners by nature, it's hard for them to admit they need love and attention. They'll rarely cop to the fact that they are unsure about anything.

But they need the support of a strong person, like you. They desperately need encouragement. He's a real puzzle. He could also be a challenge since he keeps so much inside. **Strong and silent,** he runs deep. Getting to know him is a real fishing expedition.

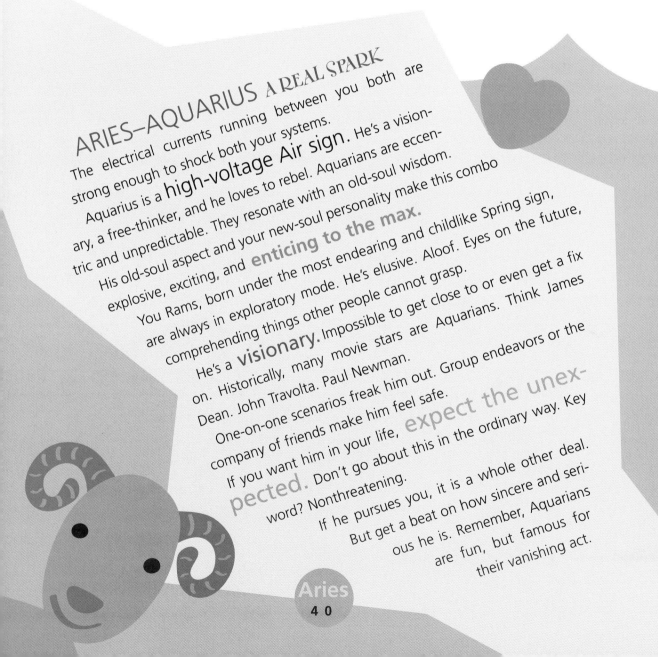

ARIES–AQUARIUS A REAL SPARK

The electrical currents running between you both are strong enough to shock both your systems. Aquarius is a **high-voltage Air sign.** He's a visionary, a free-thinker, and he loves to rebel. Aquarians are eccentric and unpredictable. They resonate with an old-soul wisdom. His old-soul aspect and your new-soul personality make this combo explosive, exciting, and **enticing to the max.**

You Rams, born under the most endearing and childlike Spring sign, are always in exploratory mode. He's elusive. Aloof. Eyes on the future, on. He's a **visionary.** Impossible to get close to or even get a fix comprehending things other people cannot grasp.

Historically, many movie stars are Aquarians. Think James Dean. John Travolta. Paul Newman.

One-on-one scenarios freak him out. Group endeavors or the company of friends make him feel safe.

If you want him in your life, **expect the unexpected.** Don't go about this in the ordinary way. Key word? Nonthreatening.

If he pursues you, it is a whole other deal. But get a beat on how sincere and serious he is. Remember, Aquarians are fun, but famous for their vanishing act.

Capricorn is synonymous with **capriciousness.** His sense of humor emerges when he feels safe. His dry wit floors you.

Since he's a winter babe, he's probably an **old soul.** He knows things. This relationship will feel more mature than most. It's based on mutual respect of your similar drive and ambition.

If you're there for him during a trying time in his life, he'll never forget it. Since he expects so little from people in general, he's always **shocked** when people do something for the sake of a good deed.

ARIES—PISCES
UNSOLVED MYSTERY

He's sensitive, psychic, and hates **confrontation.** It's impossible to know what he's feeling, mostly because he's confused himself. He's **slippery** and vague. Like the Fish.

This is in direct conflict with your Aries nature. You could end things weeks before he figures out it's over. He lives in a dream world. A fantasy-filled life.

In a better-case scenario, your **cut-to-the-chase** approach could motivate him to move. He may stop **procrastinating** so much. Don't underestimate his charm. He could turn your head and heart around so fast that you get off-track with your regular life.

He injects a sense of **unreality** into your world. He can make you more sensitive. Convince you to trust things you cannot see, like intuition, insight, and instinct. His encouragement can give you the guts to risk exposing your hidden creativity. **He believes in you.**

Pisces has too little energy to waste on betrayal. Hey, he's just trying to get out of bed before noon.

Astro Insight

His slinky and mysterious nature makes him major crush material. Even if you have a long-term thing, his mystique never fades. You'll never really know him.

MY TAROT CARD
The World

IMAGE:

A goddess is draped in a purple sash. She floats in midair, a magic wand in each hand. The fixed signs of Taurus, Leo, Scorpio, and Aquarius appear in each corner, emerging from a cosmic cloud.

MEANING:

Although Aries is a Cardinal action sign, the Fixed signs symbolize that you Rams have your eye on the ball; your mind is made up. Nothing in the world can deter you from going after what you want. You are very "fixed" in your approach.

The World equals victory. It brings recognition, results, and rewards. Guardian angels surround you, urging you to go after your goals, no matter what. It's only a matter of time until the world will be at your feet.

STAR SIBS

Matthew Broderick 3-21
Rosie O'Donnell 3-21
Reese Witherspoon 3-22
Sarah Jessica Parker 3-25
Aretha Franklin 3-25
Gloria Steinem 3-25
Elton John 3-25
Amy Smart 3-25
Steven Tyler 3-26
Diana Ross 3-26
Quentin Tarantino 3-27
Mariah Carey 3-27
Vince Vaughn 3-28
Julia Stiles 3-28
Eric Clapton 3-30
Céline Dion 3-30
Vincent van Gogh 3-30
Ewan McGregor 3-31
Al Gore 3-31
Giovanni Ribisi 3-31
Bijou Phillips 4-1

Alec Baldwin 4-3
Eddie Murphy 4-3
Marlon Brando 4-3
Maya Angelou 4-4
Heath Ledger 4-4
Natasha Lyonne 4-4
Robert Downey, Jr. 4-4
Bette Davis 4-5
Paul Rudd 4-6
Jackie Chan 4-7
Francis Ford Coppola 4-7
Russell Crowe 4-7
Haley Joel Osment 4-10
David Letterman 4-12
Claire Danes 4-12
Sarah Michelle Gellar 4-14
Lukas Haas 4-16
Conan O'Brien 4-18
Melissa Joan Hart 4-18
Kate Hudson 4-19
Ashley Judd 4-19

COSMIC ADVANTAGES

Confident
Fearless
Inventive
Assertive
Competitive
Independent
Athletic
Charismatic
Ambitious
Leader
Courageous
Daredevil
Enthusiastic
Risk-taker
Innovative
Irresistible
Passionate
Winner
Direct
Optimistic
No-nonsense
Self-reliant
Pioneer
Energetic
Self-starter
Trailblazer

COSMIC CHALLENGES

Blunt
Brutal
Abrasive
Aggressive
Destructive
Domineering
Careless
Irrational
Childish
Forceful
Rash
Egotistic
Headstrong
Impatient
Irresponsible
Sore loser
Intolerant
Reckless
Troublemaker
Hostile
Volatile
Hotheaded
Insensitive
Wild

Aries

4 4

TAURUS
APRIL 21 – MAY 19

RULING PLANET:
venus

SYMBOL:
the bull

SEASON:
spring

QUALITY:
fixed

ELEMENT:
earth

COLORS:
pistachio, kiwi, and raspberry

POWER STONES:
emerald, rose quartz

BODY:
throat, voice, and neck

FLOWERS:
violet, gerber daisy, and marigold

CITIES:
dublin, lucerne, leipzig, and cleveland

COUNTRIES:
ireland, switzerland, and iran

VIBRATION:
loyal, passionate about things i love, never quitting . . . ever!

KEY WORDS:
i am stable and seek emotional and financial prosperity.

ZODIAC HOUSE:
second

WHAT AM I LIKE?

TAURUS IS A FIXED EARTH SIGN; the most stable, steadfast sign of the Zodiac. You tend to be unusually pretty, thanks to the influence of your ruling planet Venus.

You're **sensual** and **practical**. It's what you're all about. A full-on recipe for success! You recognize your natural gifts and use them because it makes sense.

You take advantage of opportunities that come your way. You're also lucky. It's like the universe gave you a **cosmic charm bracelet** at birth. You manage to be on the receiving end of multiple lucky breaks, when you least expect them and when you need them most.

You bring great things to fruition through a Starbucks-type blend of hard work and good timing. Who ordered the Vanilla Mocha Tauruccino?

You **effortlessly attract** people who want to help you due to your magnetism, no strings attached.

"No way, I'll do it my way!" If someone tries to force you into something—

even if it's something you love to do—the typical Taurus reaction is **resistance mode.** You cannot stand being told what to do. You can be **belligerent** and **cranky** when you don't get your way. You turn into a two-year-old when someone says no and all you want to hear is yes.

This trait usually gets worse, never better, over time.

It's pure Taurus.

It's your way or no way. Okay?!!?

You're loyal, devoted, and sincere. When you say something, you mean it. It would never occur to you to bail on somebody close when they need you.

You may be slow to take action, but once you make up your mind, you're single-minded.

This is why it's so bewildering to you when people space out, flake out, or break a promise.

When serious issues occur, like betrayal, watch out. Boy, have they underestimated you! You Bulls are slow to anger, but when you get a hardcore reality check, you see red, **red,** red! Revenge is the only thing on your mind.

As a friend, you demand a lot. You expect people to deal with your difficult demands, but if they get cranky, you're the opposite of flexible. The way you see it, you're such a good friend, they're lucky to have you. It's not that you're conceited, it's just that you know your worth.

You also go nuts if you think somebody in your crowd is the favorite. You can be extremely possessive.

But on the flip side, you're **deeply loyal.** You'll do anything for a friend. Your devotion runs very deep. And people can depend on you, even if it's a hassle.

Taurus rules the voice and throat. Whether you are a musical prodigy, tone deaf, or somewhere in between, your voice is distinctive. Your soothing voice explains why you can talk anybody into anything.

If you're musical, the stars suggest you develop your gifts. Your trademark Taurus tenacity gives you the juice to practice long hours. Seek killer coaches and prestige classes. Avoid shortcuts and bad habits.

Accept it, you're a design diva. Your passion for beautiful things makes you the only family member who finds it necessary to redecorate your room on a regular basis. Your imagination is a cut above. Your creativity is inspired.

You love colors. Must-have accessories, outrageous shades of nail polish, and a daring style sense make you a favorite in winning the homeroom fashion Olympics.

You're practical. Guided by purpose and conviction, you take steps to make your dreams real. You can tune out the world when you're working on something important. You finish things.

Food, glorious food. . . . When it comes to living the good life, luxuriating in creature comforts, pampering, and pleasure seeking, Taurus rules. Food could be your number-one friend.

Like your solar opposite, Scorpio, sometimes you can feel like there is never enough. With you, there is no such thing as **too much of a good thing.**

Food could be a problem for you; metabolism, the enemy. Eating balanced meals at regular times will help you stay grounded. Sometimes you get so busy, your eating habits suffer.

Why the Bull? Centuries ago, ancient cultures depended on animals to survive. They also depended on the stars to tell them when to hunt, plant, and reap. The most valuable creatures were idolized and permanently placed in the Zodiacal belt to be eternally worshiped. A bull was one of them.

Astro Hitch

Self-sabotaging Taurus traits like indulgence and inertia can hold you hostage.

A family that owned even one bull had status. A bull was worth more then than a Porsche, Lexus, or BMW is today.

Until very recently girls were married as part of a business arrangement between families. Marry for love? You have to be kidding. A girl's family would offer up the holy, powerful bull as a portion of the wedding gift. A far cry from Williams-Sonoma and Tiffany. Bottom line, if your family owned bulls, you were considered very, very rich.

Romance-wise, you're supposed to get along with Earth and Water signs. These matches could work out, but philosophically, anyone who crosses your path is in your life for a reason. You could also feel a **spine-tingling chemistry** with the other Fixed Signs: Leo, Scorpio, and Aquarius.

Astro Tip

The Bull symbolizes wealth, good taste, power, style, and deep emotions. The Bull stands for abundance, the pleasures that life offers, and a treasure trove of inner gifts.

MY ASTRO HOUSE

TAURUS RULES THE SECOND HOUSE,

usually referred to as the money house. It refers to personal resources; material, and spiritual.

Whether you're aware of it, you Bull Babes base your "worth" on what you have. When you invest time and energy developing your gifts, it's a cosmic guarantee that you will benefit spiritually or financially. When it comes to money, you rock! You know how to save and you love to spend. You live for the good things. You're the original Material Girl. You're motivated to earn so you can buy, **buy, buy.**

You're willing to earn your own money, even if it means wearing a goofy uniform or working summers or after school. You could be the first kid to open a savings account.

You're clever at convincing your parents to boost your allowance. You point out in great detail how much you do. Your **powers of persuasion** are so good that you leave your victims in a state of shock. They don't know what hit them.

People trust you. Your cool, calm, and collected attitude ultimately leads to financial gains and emotional security from any endeavor you put your heart and soul into.

HOW DOES MY PLANETARY RULER, VENUS, AFFECT ME?

YOU "SHARE" YOUR PLANETARY RULER WITH LIBRA. This is not only confusing, but might feel unfair. Sharing anything except a ride to school is harder for you than any other sign. This state of celestial affairs could make you feel **cosmically cheated.**

This "sharing" phenomenon is actually a celestial bonus. The power of Venus manifests differently in each of you.

With **Libra,** Venus expresses itself through relationships and uses beauty as a power tool. Venus expresses herself through Taurus sensually. She rewards you when you develop your talents.

Are you the next celebrated artist? The rising star on the Hollywood circuit? A budding Olympian? The future CEO of a dot-com company? Or a college-bound Taurus, gifted with a well-deserved scholarship for the promise you've consistently shown over time?

Venus is ethereal. **Venus is the Roman goddess of love** and represents everything exquisite in the world, from physical beauty to works of art in the world's top museums.

She is physical and facial perfection. A flower that exudes an awesome bliss-you-out aroma when it blossoms. The emotion you feel when they play that song on the radio.

Venus is about connecting. Venus rules those "can't explain" feelings you get from the first flawless flush of romance. Venus gives you power to give and get love. Attracting love comes easy. You're that magnetic.

Having a soul mate, a running mate, or a stream of dates is a very important factor in your life. Goddess Venus gives you great odds when it comes to crushes.

MY FAMILY

LEO, THE SIGN OF ROYALTY AND DRAMA, governs your fourth-house cusp of family and domestic issues. You could be **to the manor born.** Your family could have money or prestige. Or, it could be dramatic, emotional, bursting with colorful characters and strong personalities.

You are **loyal, proud,** and **protective** when it comes to your immediate family. You go to great lengths to shield your weaker family members. You are always there when your family needs you. Nobody has permission to hurt your family. You shower them with things that express your sentiments. You make it your business to find the **"perfect"** gift. To you, your family is a sacred thing you take very seriously.

WHAT SHOULD I BE DOING

YOU NEED TO BE IN A FIELD YOU CAN COUNT ON. If your dreams take you into dangerous territory, like the music, money, fashion, or film business, it's only your rock-solid belief in yourself that will help you weather the storm.

People count on you. You stabilize situations. You like knowing what to expect, so you have probably researched gigs that give you a sense of control.

Intern heavily. Work in your parent's office. See what the Real World feels like.

Money intrigues you. Its power is an aphrodisiac. Your financial focus could encourage you to get an MBA.

CAREER

THE SIGN THAT GOVERNS YOUR CAREER ANGLE IN YOUR SOLAR CHART, AQUARIUS, rules TV, the media, and the Internet.

Look at the Star Sib section and see what notable Bulls have achieved. The fact that so many Tauruses are mega-stars proves that when you believe you've got what it takes to make it, a nuclear war can't stop you.

Your **"go for the gold"** attitude helps when it comes to sports. If you're good enough to make a mark for yourself when you're young, don't think opportunities will dry up when you get older. You know how to create a place for yourself when you try hard enough. It's no wonder so many professional athletes are Tauruses. With sports-specific cable outlets, sports-related magazines, and on-air commentaries from the athletic greats, the sky is the limit.

You could paint, shoot pictures, write fiction, or direct. Or you could follow the left-brain path to go pre-med or pre-law. Hard work doesn't scare you.

WITH MY LIFE?

You stick things out. You can stay in a company for a long time, prove yourself, and **climb the ladder.** You like an environment where you can form bonds and strut your stuff.

You could also find your soul mate at an early age. You like the feeling of somebody knowing the real you. Bulls need to be with people who know their history. The unfamiliar weirds you out.

Write down what you want to do, who you want to be. When things are in black and white, it makes everything more clear.

STARS TIPS ON FASHION,

MOST GIRLS WOULD LOVE A MAGIC WAND that could change them into the perfect ideal of what they're supposed to look like in order to be considered beautiful.

You're no different. You magnify imperfections until you're convinced you're such a Neanderthal you can't leave the house. **Get real!** Don't allow insecurities stop you from living your life.

With your complexion, the closer you stay to earth tones, makeup-wise, the better. Leave the flash and glitter to the Air signs!

Earthy products work **magic** undoing the stress that living on this planet creates. Herbs, homeopathic potions, and clay masks pave the way to staying gorgeous and keeping that healthy glow.

Speaking of working out—especially in a coed situation—*don't ever,* and that means ever, wear makeup when you work out.

Save makeup for parties when you know *he* will be there. Even then, most guys don't go for lots of makeup. They wonder what you're hiding.

With your hair, you benefit from botanical shampoos. Use sensible earth-derived products to enhance tone, volume, and flexibility. When it comes to your cut and style, **speak up** when you want to change your look.

Don't follow the mall rats. Instead, make sure you have **the classics:** black fitted pants, a button-down shirt, and that perfect thrift-store jacket.

Baby pink, periwinkle blue, azure, sapphire, and cobalt offset all that hardcore black that never goes out of style. Go for tones that enhance your eyes. You Bulls need to feel comfortable, so make sure the colors you wear are never wearing you!

Regarding your health: remember that Taurus rules the voice, throat, and neck. Protect these vulnerable areas and adorn your throat in mystical, intriguing necklaces.

HEALTH, AND BEAUTY

You're aware that your passion for food could become a problem. Watch out that your lazybones mode doesn't turn into a full-time job. Even if it's just walking the dog, being outside clears your head.

CUSP KIDZ

ARIES-TAURUS: APRIL 18–22

You cuspers possess **daring** and **stamina.** The Aries inside seeks the fresh, the new, and the unknown. The Taurus inside gives you the staying power to take your discoveries to their natural conclusion.

Power is your middle name. This is the **Cusp of Courage.** The Aries inventor blends with the Taurus soldier who never quits. It's a mind-blowing combination of astrological forces.

You find gold at the rainbow's end. You know how to increase what you have and make things last. You **think big and act bold.** You attract things that give you security.

Security is your objective. It's like oxygen.

TAURUS-GEMINI: MAY 18–22

The power of an incoming sign overshadows the influence of the outgoing sign. If you are at the end of your Sun sign, you are deeply affected by next Sun sign.

In your case, however, it's a little different. You Taurus fems are so **stubborn, territorial, and Bullish** about being a Taurus that you hang on with your fingernails to maintain your Taurus identity.

But this cusp is so cool, it won't be so hard to shift gears and embrace the dual nature of your identity. This is the **Cusp of Success.**

The Taurus in you has extraordinary powers of concentration.

Add the verbal gifts of a Gemini to this recipe and you hit a home run.

TAURUS–TAURUS
BULLFIGHT OR TOGETHER FOREVER?

This same sign combination can be one of those "boy meets girl, boy loses girl, boy gets girl" romances. On one hand, you cannot get enough of each other, but when you butt heads, you go to your corners and stomp your feet until you get your way. **You're both willing to risk everything** to be right. Even if it means breaking up. This is where you start playing Truth or Dare. Do you dare be the first one to admit you're wrong? Can you feel safe enough to tell the truth?

Are you willing to learn something about yourself through this relationship? Face facts, girl! He has your attention. You may actually consider another point of view . . . his. He could be **the one person** who teaches you the difference between being right and alone or compromising to be together. You both have your feet on the ground and know where you want to go. You're both pleasure seekers and love creature comforts.

You can be yourself with him, hang out, and not flip out trying to impress him. He likes you as you are.

Most guys roam and hunt, but when he finds what he likes, he hangs out to see where it's going to go. Even if you eventually split, his loyal Taurus streak makes it possible to stay friends.

Be certain you're **sure** before getting involved. He will pick up on your clues and take you seriously. He can be even more persistent than you.

If you tease too much, his nostrils will flare and you'll have a real situation on your hands. Add to the mix his bursting-at-the-seams Taurus ego and you have a real **heavyweight** on your hands. This bond comes under the category of "When it's good, it's great, but when it goes south, duck!"

TAURUS–GEMINI
SPRING FEVER

This combo can be a hit, miss, or one-hit wonder because your personalities are so different.

You Taurus fems are **solid earth.** You like to know what to expect. Always grounded, you can always be counted on. Surprises are not really your thing.

But when a Gemini drops unexpectedly into your life, **chaos reigns.** He's too cute to get mad at, but can also drive you nuts. Flakes give you hives. He'll bail too many times, and it will drive you mad.

While you're fuming, he's onto his next adventure, oblivious to the fact that he did anything wrong. Meet Mr. No Attention Span! He's in constant motion, needs plenty of room, and even more "space." He's an Air sign, an airhead, and hard to pin down.

He can talk you into anything and talk himself out of anything.

He actually believes what he says while he's saying it, but he can forget what he said in less than an hour. **Amazing.**

He absolutely sparkles at the beginning, when things are shiny and new. He'll have you walking on air. But, he can lack the capacity to keep things going in a meaningful way in the long haul.

But if you're in a **crush coma,** here's heavenly news. You share the same seasonal vibration. The odds are good that you have planets in Gemini or he has a few in Taurus. If this is the case, his flightiness might not be so unmanageable and your earthiness might be just the thing he's looking for.

Astro Tip

Don't wait around for Peter Pan to grow up. You will quickly discover if he is all talk or the real deal.

TAURUS–CANCER PASSION MEETS COMPASSION

This is a traditional Earth–Water coupling that is supposed to be successful since your Suns form the aspect of opportunity. In this **elemental enchilada,** Water (Cancer) nourishes Earth (Taurus).

Cancer is a **touchy-feely,** moody, and emotional sign. In our society, it's fine for girls to get achy-breaky hearts or spend weeks analyzing a look, but it's not okay for a guy to do this.

When a guy exhibits any form of weakness to his peers, he runs the risk of being cast out, laughed at, and being called a wimp.

Consider the Cancerian's astrological symbol: Crab-hard exterior with mush inside. Then there's the way crabs move . . . backward. Heavy metaphors.

Cancerians are security-minded. For him to make the first move and risk rejection is a huge deal.

Get used to being the **initiator.** Not that he isn't a doer, but he can get so convoluted and turn into a land mine of emotions. He just needs a nudge.

But relationships are a two-way street and you should not be doing all the work.

Talk frankly. Choose your language carefully. He is Water and all about emotion; always use the word "feel" when you're around him. This holds true with the other two Water signs as well.

TAURUS–VIRGO THE REAL DEAL

Virgo is one of the most misunderstood signs of the Zodiac. Virgos are unpredictable, intelligent, and independent. They're always thinking, plotting, and **planning.** They live in a world of facts and figures and are constantly judging what they see. If you were to get inside their heads, it would be like walking into the CNN studios.

Virgos are precise, finicky, and have plenty of eccentricities. He's **Mr. Organization.** He loves to dissect and analyze things.

Even though he's an Earth sign, he's not touch-feely. He's cerebral. He has this compulsion for order and technique. He could seem a little cold on the romantic front. He's not very emotional. For all you know he could be desperately in love even though he's never said a thing.

TAURUS–LEO
THE DYNAMIC DUO

Earth meets Fire. But it is more than that. Two massive forces of nature collide on planet Earth and from then on, hold onto your seat! You are both "fixed" signs, a **red flag** that signals serious chemistry.

Since you're Spring and he's Summer, you both have **energy to burn.** When you lay eyes on each other, there's an irresistible force pulling you two together.

You are both **practical.** You don't waste time with silly things that lead nowhere. This extends to your relationship. You will know fast if this love match will last. Neither of you exactly holds back.

You speak a language

you both understand. He can help you figure out the meaning of things. He's a great advice giver and very fair.

He's quirky and finicky. He has plenty of pet peeves. If you try too hard to please him, forget it. In terms of **the Big Picture,** he is a realist. If the initial attraction fades, he's somebody you want to keep in your life.

If you are at the beginning of this romance dance, here are a few pointers. The Lion is exciting, but he needs plenty of stroking. **Translation?**

He could be more of a project than you expected. If he's worth it, you won't mind as long as he appreciates the time and effort you're putting in.

Leos are generous, whether they can afford to do something or not. If he's withholding, that's a good indication of his lack of interest. If it's apparent it's a one-way street and you're doing all the driving, tell him to **get out of the car and walk!**

If you're talking to your girlfriends more than you're talking to him, you have a problem. If you're talking to him more than you're talking to your friends, you have a relationship.

If he's all flash, talking trash, and throwing around the cash, that's **a real turnoff.** Being loud masks his insecurities. Why let him act out on your time?

TAURUS–LIBRA
GORGEOUS AND GRATIFYING

This combo can be **a slice of heaven** in your earthy world. The key to compatibility is educating yourself in the language of Libra because you don't like surprises.

Your Libra love interest is one of the more beautiful people. He's a master at getting what he wants. In this case, it could be you.

This may start slow since you resist change and he cannot make up his mind. You share **stunning Venus** as your ruler, which heightens the romance of this love match. You could also be a great-looking couple.

You may be the one who always wants to solidify things. Who is never quite sure where things are headed.

This is where Air and Earth part ways. He's more comfortable with the concept of being together than doing the necessary work to really become a couple. But don't be too hard on him.

He's a **die-hard romantic** and will absolutely lose himself in the fantasy of it all. You'll truly feel touched by an angel. But angels are ethereal. He could **vanish** when the pressure mounts. The harder you try to make things work, the further he'll drift. It's so hard for him to **commit.** You could be long gone before he figures out that what he really wanted was you.

TAURUS–SAGITTARIUS
EARTH GIRL MEETS JET-SETTER

Sagittarius is the most spiritual sign of the Zodiac and probably one of the most physically active. Sagittarians are free-spirited, fun loving, and perpetual students of life. They love travel, whether it's inside their head by studying or a last-minute hop to Europe. They are on a spiritual quest.

Full of bravado, he'll give you the kind of adrenaline rush you get in a red Mustang, top down, wind flying through your hair. He's always manages to get into the ultimate parties with the cool crowd at all times.

There's something about the **Archer male** that makes people want to be around him. His life is one episode after

TAURUS–SCORPIO
PASSION PLAY

Your solar opposite, Scorpio, pulls you in so deep you can barely breathe. Talk about a **cosmic challenge!**

He can be manipulative, noble, or saintly. No matter what form he takes, he'll teach you more about life and love than you expected or even wanted.

Scorpians come into this world with **difficult karma.** They internalize. Their waters run deep. They don't take things lightly. They're hypersensitive. They look for the deeper meaning of things.

His sexuality is undeniable. They pull you in to their force field and **hypnotize** you.

You can be a positive influence on your solar opposite. You see things for what they are. You can shake him out of his intensity. His emotional tidal waves can literally drown him. You are the island he escapes to from the storm.

He's high-maintenance. When you're not under his spell, ask yourself if he's worth the trouble. Are you getting as much as you're giving?

Your job? Be straight up. Talk to him. Tell him what you need. He's **no mind reader.** Know when he's asking too much.

Keep things light. You'll need your girlfriends to ground you while you two hang out.

another, like a lifelong miniseries. He doesn't take things too seriously. You should understand that you're his costar right now, but the cast is sure to change.

Unless there are modifying planetary placements, you'll soon discover how different you two are. You play for keeps. He keeps on playing. This can be fun for a while.

A good idea for you Earth girls with this Shooting Star? Enjoy it while it lasts. He hates when things get too heavy. The fun side of you needs a Sag in your life. He's provocative and a born philosopher.

When it comes to romance, he's Mr. Good-Time, all the time. It's rare to find a depressed Sag. He's too busy with the business of living to let anything get him down. He likes to keep things positive.

So, even if you have a short-lived fling, he'll want to stay friends. He'll be delighted if you call him.

TAURUS–AQUARIUS
STABLE MEETS UNAVAILABLE

You are in for the **ride of your life** with the most elusive, unavailable Zodiac male. Every Taurus loves a challenge and, boy, have you found one. You are both Fixed signs, which can be good or bad, depending on the day.

When you agree on something, a **nuclear war** can't get you to change your minds. But if you both disagree, it could be weeks before either of you picks up the phone.

TAURUS–CAPRICORN TRUE BLUE

Earth to Earth can work, but the Capricorn male is one of the most **complicated** creatures on Planet Earth. The question is, are you up for the job? And more importantly, can he give you the things you need and deserve?

Typically, Capricorns are late bloomers. They're full-on winter. As a result, they **isolate** and **hibernate**. They're patient and ambitious—a lethal combination.

Plus, they need love so badly, but their tough exterior prevents them from asking for what they most need.

You're both Earth in search of stability. You can give this to each other. Since you are spring, your upbeat attitude gives him a welcome reprieve from his **doom-and-gloom** thinking.

Capricorns get younger as they get older—it's the Saturn effect. But at your age, he can seem to have the weight of the world on his shoulders.

He's sly and cagey and won't reveal his plans. In fact, he could have singled you out already as his **perfect soul mate.** But does he show any sign of this? Of course not! His fear of rejection runs so deep, it is up to you to give him the thumbs-up and encourage him to open his mouth.

On the other side, his old soul self can teach you a thing or two about making things last.

When this love match works, there's nothing like a Capricorn guy **opening his heart** and soul to you.

He deals in **honesty.** The trick to making this work is not trying too hard. Be yourself. Don't try to impress him. Either he likes what he sees or he doesn't. The same goes for you.

His appeal comes from his individuality and inventive thinking. **He's one in a million.**

Air signs hate feeling trapped or manipulated. And they pick up on that stuff right away. Starting things off on a friendship level is the best thing to do. Aquarians shy away from the one-on-one thing.

TAURUS–PISCES INFATUATION AND INTRIGUE

This combo could be the stuff dreams are made of. Pisces is a sensitive, poetic, and psychic sign. The Fish is not afraid of his emotions, like most of the male population.

Most of the world's greatest actors, musicians, and comedians are born under the sign of Pisces. This sign is **prophetic** and mystic. Also, many famous scientists have Pisces prominent in their chart. So how does this affect you?

Even on a good day, he has one foot on this planet and the other in outer space. He loves to party and does not know when to stop. That's where you come in. Your **stabilizing** energy makes him feel **rooted.** Like he has a purpose. Plus, you both have an **artistic** side.

He's an isolator. If he's a musician, he could lock himself in his garage practicing guitar until his fingers bleed. If he writes, he'll hide out until his manuscript is done. He has a problem with boundaries. He can't see them.

You see **his potential.** He listens to you. He believes that you believe in him. He feeds your soul. He has the emotional resources to cope with the insecurities and defenses you've developed.

Water nourishes Earth and keeps it alive. But you give him form. You give him a reason to believe that things can work out.

TAURUS–ARIES
SEASONAL AND SIZZLING

Despite your elemental differences—Earth and Fire—the odds of having personal **planetary harmony** are high.

Your Goddess Venus Vibration, the essential female spirit with his oh-so-masculine Mars makes an **unbeatable** mixture. You give each other goose bumps. Your earthy sensuality keeps him coming back.

You are both in the same season. You have a similar sense of **right** and **wrong,** want similar things from life, and have the necessary energy to get where you want to go. Up!

The yin-yang vibration is a thing of beauty. An Aries male is truly masculine and makes you swoon. Your trademark Taurus stubborn streak goes right out the window around him. He has that kind of effect.

And how do you affect him? He'll never tell. He's an action figure. Watch what he does, not what he says.

Better to get a solid something in the romance department than a bunch of sweet nothings.

Most Aries guys are **nonverbal.** It's hard for them to even make small talk when they are with their buddies.

Athletic to the point of obsession, it can't hurt if you are a sports nut. But don't force it. If you hate football, or think baseball is boring to watch, don't try to pretend. You're no good at it.

The **good news** is that neither of you wastes time on the wrong person.

The "wrong" Aries has a mean temper. He can be **brash, rash,** and insensitive. If you start fighting, don't wait around. It's not going to get better. Period.

MY TAROT CARD
Strength

IMAGE:

Dressed in pure white, the goddess calmly holds a lion's head. The symbol of Infinity crowns her. A flowering wreath is woven in her hair. A rugged landscape lies behind her.

MEANING:

Strength is not about muscle mass. It's about taming negative forces inside. It's about befriending scary feelings. Strength tells you life doesn't need to be as hard as you make it out to be. It promises that you will always have what it takes to walk through any obstacle that comes your way.

STAR SIBS

Charlotte Brontë 4-21
Andie MacDowell 4-21
Queen Elizabeth II 4-21
Jack Nicholson 4-22
Meryl Streep 4-22
William Shakespeare 4-23
Shirley Temple Black 4-23
Barbra Streisand 4-24
Djimon Hounsou 4-24
Shirley MacLaine 4-24
Al Pacino 4-25
Renée Zellweger 4-25
Jessica Alba 4-28
Penélope Cruz 4-28
Jay Leno 4-28
Jerry Seinfeld 4-29
Daniel Day-Lewis 4-29
André Agassi 4-29
Michelle Pfeiffer 4-29
Uma Thurman 4-29
Kirsten Dunst 4-30
Lance Bass 5-4
George Clooney 5-6

Amy Heckerling 5-7
Enrique Iglesias 5-8
Linda Evangelista 5-10
Bono 5-10
Fred Astaire 5-10
Jason Biggs 5-12
Stephen Baldwin 5-12
Katharine Hepburn 5-12
Ving Rhames 5-12
Samantha Mathis 5-12
Harvey Keitel 5-13
Stevie Wonder 5-13
Dennis Rodman 5-13
Cate Blanchette 5-14
George Lucas 5-14
Chazz Palminteri 5-15
Janet Jackson 5-16
Tori Spelling 5-16
Omar Epps 5-16
Gabrielle Sabatini 5-16
Trent Reznor 5-17
Dennis Hopper 5-17
Bill Paxton 5-17

COSMIC ADVANTAGES

Affectionate

Good-hearted

Productive

Stable

Artistic

Grounded

Prosperous

Creative

Security-minded

Steadfast

Loyal

Deep

Substantial

Faithful

Passionate

Sensual

Patient

Supportive

Funny

Practical

Serene

Gentle

Thorough

COSMIC CHALLENGES

Truthful

Jealous

Lazy

Bullheaded

Clinging

Possessive

Depressive

Needy

Obstinate

Procrastinator

Envious

Suspicious

Extravagant

Selfish

Greedy

Overbearing

Self-seeking

Territorial

Overindulgent

Vindictive

Inhibited

Grudge-holder

Pessimistic

Stubborn

GEMINI

MAY 20 – JUNE 20

RULING PLANET:
mercury

SYMBOL:
the twins

SEASON:
spring

QUALITY:
mutable

ELEMENT:
air

COLORS:
daffodil yellow, apricot, hot pink, and periwinkle blue

POWER STONES:
aquamarine, amber

BODY:
hands, arms, and nervous system

FLOWERS:
bird of paradise, peony, and orange blossom

CITIES:
london, boston, san francisco, and melbourne

COUNTRIES:
wales, belgium, u.s.a.

KEY WORDS:
i think and talk a lot. every-thing fascinates me . . . for a while!

ZODIAC HOUSE:
third

VIBRATION:
inquisitive and changeable

WHAT AM I LIKE?

GEMINI IS THE SIGN OF THE FLIRT, dilettante, inventor, muse, author, and communicator.

This may sound corny, but Geminis are the Zodiac's **fairy princesses,** sprites, elves, pixies, nymphs, and all the magical creatures that populate this earth. It's like you've been sprinkled with cosmic fairy dust. You live in a magical world colored by your unique way of thinking.

You're **two people in one,** which is why you're called the Twin. But, you may feel that you have more than two sides.

Gemini is associated with the Greek god Hermes, son of Zeus. Known as the **messenger** of the gods, he led souls to the gates of Hades, the Greek underworld.

Hermes was the god of travel, luck, music, eloquence, commerce, younger men, and thieves. He was said to have invented the **lyre** and the **flute.** He's equated with the Roman god Mercury.

You **pen the poetry,** design the play, define the drama, or don the mask of tragedy or comedy. Inventive, communicative, and easily bored, you are champagne aristocrats in a world of beer-guzzling slackers.

You are a **Divine Discontent.**

Even when something good happens, you always think it could be better. You **secretly enjoy** being frustrated because it gives you something to do.

You're bored being with one person all the time, so it's important to cultivate as many friends as possible. Friends help you feel **connected** to the world. You're not shy and will talk to anyone. In fact, sometimes you work out your anxiety by rambling on in a stream of consciousness. You always have a cell phone attached to your ear.

You'll find **any** reason to talk to anyone at **anytime.**

Sometimes your brain works so fast, you don't even finish your sentences. Your organizer book can have more contacts, friends, and acquaintances than the telephone book. Your friendships can be superficial because you spread yourself so thin.

Your verbal skills are superb. Talking makes you feel safe. To you, an idea is a possession. The Gemini equation is "I think, therefore I am."

The evolved Gemini is never about what she has,

but always about what she knows.

Never satisfied with one thing for long, you **personify the butterfly** that flits from flower to flower, riveted by the transitory brilliance of the color of the sun.

Gemini seeks completion through union. But this sensation is fleeting. You lack the capacity to handle commitments and flee from responsibility. This conflict can dog you for years. If you *do* find someone who meets your romance **requirements**, control your impulse to run away.

Your birth season provides undeniable parallels to your personality. The May–June period marks the traditional wedding season. A time that celebrates the mystical union of two souls. Subconsciously, you strive to recreate the rapture associated with the honeymoon phase over and over again.

It is central to your personal theme to perpetually search for your other half.

MY ASTRO HOUSE

THE THIRD HOUSE REPRESENTS THE CONSCIOUS MIND, early education, communication, interaction, how you take in information, and how you learn. You could be an avid reader, a born teacher, a media maven, a gifted writer, or just a plain old chatterbox.

Your early education and the friends from that time will always have a special place in your **heart** and mind. You may even stay in touch with your friends from elementary school long into adulthood.

The **third house** also represents short trips, siblings, errands, and your neighborhood. Short trips involve phone calls, lists, and short-term strategy—all areas where you **excel**. Your birthday month is also a vacation month—a time for family reunions. This is all third-house stuff.

HOW DOES MY PLANETARY RULER, MERCURY, AFFECT ME?

YOUR RULING PLANET MERCURY governs all forms of **communication,** the ability to understand the world around you, and the power to absorb information.

Mercury governs the upper extremities. You use your hands, fingers, and arms to emphasize a point. These **enhance** your ability to communicate.

Mercury also governs the **nervous system.** Signals to your brain through your nervous system allow you to react, think, and move. You tend to be high-strung and wound very tight.

Luckily, you know when you are about to reach **critical** mass. That's when you call your **friends** for a reality check—before the committee between your ears takes control.

MY FAMILY

PERFECTIONIST, finicky Virgo is on your **fourth-house cusp** of home and family. Virgo is erratic and changeable, so different situations are possible.

Virgo is all about precision, science, health, **work,** and **service.** Translation? Your home can be a place of learning. Of charity. Of doing what is right. Your parents will try to drill ethics, morals, and proper actions into your head. They will tell you **exactly** what it takes to be appropriate and be a good person.

It's likely that one or both parents work in the health or service field.

A doctor, nurse, pediatrician, or civil servant.

Since Virgo is a **volatile vibration,** there could be divorce, perhaps more than one. In this case, your siblings become very important. You depend on them and they can count on you. In fact, your parents could become so unavailable that your **siblings** become your entire world. There could be a role-reversal with your parents in this case.

You may be **thrust** into taking adult responsibilities long before you're supposed do.

WHAT SHOULD I BE DOING

SEEK A JOB OR CAREER THAT REQUIRES THE BRAINPOWER OF TEN. Look for an environment that depends on ingenious, innovative thinking. **Stagnation makes you crazy.**

You are a cosmic spy sent into situations that depend on your smarts. You will find yourself placed in positions of increasingly greater responsibility where your brainpower is essential.

CAREER

MANY GEMINIS ARE SEDUCED into the actor's life. Playful, comedic, and usually gorgeous, you depict those people who lead a charmed life. The lifestyle entices you flighty Twins. An actor's life can be frustrating, but it is never dull. Always a new coach, love interest, project, location, scene partner, or character to create.

In fashion, there's always something new and everything changes. Always a new season, sale, collection, boutique. Everything is young, hip, and glamorous.

You can be a buyer, do marketing, book models, or start out as a window dresser. You are part of a system that feeds on originality and new ideas.

The publicist ranks as an almost perfect Gemini job. It demands wizardry. You create the image; invent the heat. You dance between the artist's reps and the demanding public. You manipulate the media, deal with mega-egos on a bihourly basis, and resolve dramas with diplomacy. One minute you do damage control, the next, you provide perks to the cultural elite.

As a writer, you have a direct line to the celestial Muse. Speak the truth or entertain the world. There's always a story to tell, someone to fictionalize, another drama to design, another incident to provide comic relief.

Then there's music. Divas, MTV personalities, musicians, video directors, A and R execs, VJs, DJs, roadies, groupies, background singers, lyricists, rock 'n' roll managers, critics, record store employees. These are just a few players who make the recording industry spin.

Songs are short enough not to tax your short attention span.

WITH MY LIFE?

When things get too real, too serious, or too heavy, you are out the door. A memory. Your winged feet have already left the ground.

$1500

$950

$3,000

STARS TIPS ON FASHION,

BEGINNING GOOD HABITS NOW PROLONGS YOUR CELESTIALLY YOUTHFUL APPEARANCE.
Your enthusiastic, almost adolescent mind-set keeps you young.

Do things, like **yoga,** that dissolve stress caused by anxiety. Use Gemini's powerful planetary image for meditation purposes. Mercury is the active ingredient in the thermometer. You also take temperatures—moral, spiritual, ethical, and emotional. When you feel things get too hot, you run.

Mercury is formless, morphing into its container's shape. Elusive to human touch, its movement is surreal. Its silvery, fluid energy can help you evolve into your most intuitive state. Use this as a mental symbol.

Mercury **rules the lungs.** Breathing is the most important thing to develop awareness of in your everyday life. Proper breathing stimulates essential endorphins, integrates the mind-body-spirit triad, and is crucial to long-term well-being.

You can wear just about any **color.** Bright, vivid colors usually perk you up. Indulge in shades of yellow like saffron, lemon mist, tawny, khaki, tan, wheat, fawn, sienna—or heart-stopping fuchsias or indigos. Wear things that interest you.

AS FOR HAIR,
you need an interesting "do," because your hands, unconsciously or not, always end up playing with your hair. Adapt seasonally. Style should reflect your mood. Scrunchies are always fun. Keep hair off your face to avoid those nasty oily pores.

Wear whatever makes you feel **airborne** and **flirtatious**. Be the gypsy queen with a swirly skirt, tight top, and romantic scarf. Or tone it down with faded Levi's, boots, and a button-down shirt to keep them guessing.

There are so many fun beauty products out there in the market, it could make you dizzy. Whether it's a trendy MAC foundation or a sensible Clinique regime for urban air, have plenty of choices.

HEALTH, AND BEAUTY

Maintain a disciplined regime with your cleansers and conditioners. You must have **travel-size** products, because you're always on the go. Keep your backpack and locker stashed. Just remember to throw out dried-out funky makeup when it's older than you!

CUSP KIDZ

TAURUS–GEMINI: MAY 18–22

This cusp produces a highly effective individual because it combines the best of both worlds: the grounded, sensuous Bull with the capricious, clever Twin. Taurus's "keep your eye on the ball" attitude tones down the Twin's low or no attention span. The success rate attributed to people born on this cusp ranks high. This is the **Cusp of the Muse.** Earthy vibration intermingles with an imaginative approach. You attract guys without lifting a fingernail. Your hardest task? Deciding who to eliminate.

You cuspers care deeply about the things you love (Taurus) but have the **spark** to expand your world (Gemini).

GEMINI–CANCER: JUNE 18–22

People born on this cusp lead the Charmed Life. Historically, people on this cusp are leaders. Your social skills are top-notch. People feel lucky to be around you. You are born with sparkle. To be born within the orb of the summer solstice gives you an unmistakable charisma. This is the **Cusp of Charisma.** With love, the sky is the limit. And you have plenty of choices. Your flirtation skills were polished before you turned ten. You are so fast on the uptake that you never suffer fools for long. Your "can't wait to make it happen" energy gives you a gift for the game of love.

Gemini can be accused of moving on too quickly when something bores them. You're not wicked, you just get **antsy.** Add to this mix Cancer's sensitivity, perception, and intuition of a Moonchild, and you come up a winner.

COSMIC LOVE MATCHES

GEMINI–GEMINI
ON YOUR TOES

The male Twin hates when things get too serious. He tries to extract the most fun from each situation at all times. This same-sign bond could have **a long life span** because you always keep each other guessing. When you're together, there's an element of escapism you both enjoy. Since you both love to travel, expect to do, go, see, and connect to the world as a couple. This matchup could be a **together-forever** kind of thing. Your shared experiences fuse your relationship. You are equally intelligent. You may be smart about different things, but that is even more reason to hang out or study together.

Not only will you end up helping each other, but also you won't make each other feel inadequate or stupid.

With romance, keep things loose and easy. **Start as friends.** Get to know him.

Whether it's you or him, you Twins are captivating. Your "little black books" overflow with the names of a million friends. When you're not seriously dating, you probably have more than fifteen guys who'd love to take you out.

He probably has the same amount of girls "in waiting." But pay attention. He's a **mischiefmaker** and loves to lead a double life. He may sneak behind your back. If you get that funky vibe *and* he starts to come up with lame excuses, flee the scene immediately.

Astro Hint

Guys aren't as complicated as you think.

GEMINI–LEO
DELICIOUS DISH

When this love match works, you'll pinch yourself to make sure you're awake. Leo gives you the kind of love and affection that makes you feel skyrocketed to the **galaxy of Party Central.** You're both social, popular, and love to have fun. You're **cosmically programmed** to extract the maximum amount of pleasure in the shortest period of time. You insist on enjoying yourself and so does the Lion. When you're in crush mode, your world consists of him and you. Period. Nobody else exists.

GEMINI–CANCER
FLIRTATION SENSATION

This can be a very interesting and successful combination. A Moonchild possesses **sensitivity** and **intuition.** Plus, you're back-to-back signs, and the odds are good you share planets conducive to a lasting love.

You **intrigue** him more than he'll let on. Concealment is a Cancer trait to be aware of. He's cagey and keeps to himself. He is so secretive that figuring him out could become a full-time project.

Your Cancer will do everything in his power to make you happy. He sees it as protecting his investment. He likes what he has and doesn't want to lose it.

It takes **forever** to earn his trust. By the time he steps up to the plate, it may be too late. You've probably gone the distance with somebody else by the time he realizes he should have made his move. **You hate to wait!**

He knows how to play it and how to play you. Before you know it, you could find yourself doing things—like his laundry (yuck!)—that you don't even do for yourself. They have a way of making you feel guilty.

If this linkup becomes more about his needs than yours, find the door.

Astro Trap

The Lion is fiercely loyal and can't handle betrayal or losing face.

His fire sparks your interest about life. He is free of petty things. He's demonstrative, loves to play host, and show you off.

The Lion loves flattery and adoration. If anybody can rise to the occasion, it's you. When it comes to telling him how he makes you feel, you actually enjoy doing it.

With your notoriously short attention span, you could be a **real heartbreaker** if you lose interest. There's no way around it, breakups are always hard whether you're the Dumper or the Dumpee. If you want to move on, be gentle. You just may permanently crush his ego if you're not careful.

GEMINI–VIRGO
PRACTICALLY PERFECT

This love match is **uncommonly interesting.** Even though he's Earth and you're Air, you both share Mercury as a ruling planet and have the same Mutable quality.

This makes you "transitional" signs. Your function is to convert one season's energy into the next. You change spring to summer. He changes summer to fall. You're both adaptable, quick thinkers, and love variety.

He can match you word for word. You give each other food for thought and make great study buds. You're both so **smart,** you can always figure a way out of any relationship problem. He dissects what is already there. You come up with fresh ways to deal with an old situation.

His **earthy practicality** helps ground you. Left to your own devices, you'd bail on the books if you heard about a party.

GEMINI–LIBRA
TICKETS TO PARADISE

Be careful what you wish for, because boy did you strike gold. You have been given a **first-class ticket to nirvana** with the man of your dreams. This combination is what romance novels are made of.

The best part is that both of you are **committed** to making this relationship work. The trine aspect that is formed between your Suns creates a predominantly pleasant atmosphere with little danger of getting into a fight.

Libra is the **relationship sign.** He takes on the attributes and qualities of the person he's with. Around you, he becomes

GEMINI–SCORPIO AN INTENSE MIX

His intensity may be too much for you to take, even if you're attracted to him. He can pull you into a **vortex of emotion** that causes you to lose balance and forget where you are. But if **Mr. Sexy** suddenly drops into your life, steel yourself. There's nothing boring or trivial about this. He scares you but intrigues you. A Scorpio has such heavy-duty karma, you sense your relationship has a purpose, a message, and **direction.**

the attraction—besides the obvious (think Leonardo, Jeremy London, Jason Scott Lee, and Ethan Hawke . . . *hello!*)—is your compulsion to always figure everything out.

Scorpio **transforms.** Once you lock lips, he's already managed to change you. He makes you feel things you didn't even know were possible.

His feelings are easily hurt and he does hold a grudge. If you see things are going down fast, **protect yourself.**

Figure out a way to *have him* break up with you; it's less dangerous. If there's any fast-talking Zodiac sign, **baby, it's you!**

Since you are a solid member of the spring set, part of

even more charming and devil-may-care. He can be strangely detached and unemotional, like you. He is **enamored** by how witty and pretty you are.

He's **romantic.** He will get lost in you. The only thing better than a Libra in love is a Libra in love with you.

Astro Glitch

Libra's special brand of narcissism could really turn you off.

GEMINI–SAGITTARIUS
THE BIG PICTURE

This bond is **pure bliss.** You both love life, learning, and the pursuit of happiness. Together, you're a walking **Declaration of Independence.**

But you see the Small Picture and he sees the Big Picture, so you end up balancing each other out.

You live for the **adrenaline rush** of romance. You jump in feet first, never thinking things through. When you like what you see, that's all you need.

He is **prone to exaggeration**

and gets bored just like you. This can be entertaining, but it can also get old **quick.**

The one catch that could make this a short-term thing is your equally short attention spans. Sag is all about **motion**—getting on with the business of his life. And you most likely have more guys interested in you than you know what to do with. **Overnight,** both of you could simply lose interest and move on. You won't be hurting long.

GEMINI–CAPRICORN
BUBBLY AND EFFERVESCENT

This is an **unlikely combination** most people believe can't work. Not so. This is probably one of the more interesting and **unbeatable** linkups around.

Mr. Impenetrable benefits from your bubbly personality. You remind

him life isn't so serious.

And what can he do for you? **Plenty.** Once you get past his **shy routine,** which is simply a test to make sure that you—Ms. Popularity—really really like him, you can get on with the business of building a relationship. His stone-cold sober exterior may deter you, but you can get under his

GEMINI–AQUARIUS
SMART, SAVVY, AND SOPHISTICATED

Your Sun signs create a **lucky trine aspect** that can lead to love. He can deal with your flighty, flirty tendency. You can deal with his aloof attitude. You make intellectual contact with sophistication and style.

Maybe you're scared to let your hair down. Maybe it's hard to get serious because your feelings always change. Maybe you can't deal with confrontations. He can relate.

He's savvy and sophisticated. He may seem more **mature** and **spiritual.** He calms down your nerves.

Your Aquarian keeps you on your toes because he satisfies your need for variety. He's unpredictable. And vice versa. When you're around him, you are on your best behavior, which is a very atypical thing for you to do.

There's something about the way he makes you feel that has you seriously thinking about ways to make this last.

skin, whether he admits it or not.

Capricorns know how to wait. He plays for keeps. He could actually say something along the lines of "I know you're seeing other guys, but you're probably not going to find anyone who will care about you like I can. I'm not going anywhere."

Once you **get over the shock** of hearing such an admission, you'll probably come to your senses. He is telling you that he could be the Mr. Right instead of the Mr. Right Now.

He can be **serious** and **dark.** He's winter and most winter babies are old souls. They know things. Why not learn?

GEMINI–PISCES
A MYSTICAL ADVENTURE

This may seem to be an **unusual** linkup on the surface, but the fact that you are both Mutable signs is an **astrological bonus.**

You deal in facts, logic, and reason. He deals with dreams, what-ifs, and fantasies. You are a **thinker.** He is an emotional visionary. But even though your orientations to the world are different, you both have **dual energies.**

The symbol of Pisces is two Fish swimming in opposite directions. **Meaning?** He is usually in a state of confusion and always of two minds, which is something you can certainly relate to.

GEMINI–ARIES
LOVE IS BLIND

This love match could **change your life.** You're both dynamic. Together you could be in Bliss City for a long time. He's **fire** and you're **air.** Meaning? Your windy vibration only makes him hotter. Just make sure you can deal with his heat because there is going to be plenty of passion—more in store than even you can possibly imagine. You are both born with **matchless vitality,** spring spirit, and are always on the go. Things to watch out for on both sides?

He angers so fast, you won't know what you did. You'll have to put on a helmet to dodge the bullets. Know that his moods have nothing to do with you. You happen to be the only one in the room. An Aries male is straight-forward, direct, and has **no time to waste.** He needs to win and is very hard on himself. If you take things personally, he can really burst your self-esteem bubble. You hate being tied down to just one thing. Geminis have emotional **claustrophobia.** An Aries–Gemini bond has a very good chance of working out. But the timing could be off. Remember, it's the holding on that hurts.

When you guys get confused, you handle it differently. He tries to get a fix on how he feels but has a difficult time thinking things through.

This is where you **can help.** You are an idea person and can see a situation from more than one angle. You see things that never occured to him.

On the other side, he is so **sexy** and sensitive he could help you deal with your emotions. He opens your eyes to the more artistic side of life. It would be just like a love-struck Pisces to take you on a picnic, not caring whether or not it's "cool." He doesn't care what anyone thinks.

GEMINI–TAURUS
PATIENCE IS A VIRTUE

This **seasonal blend** of energies is a basketful of delightful surprises because you are you not supposed to get along. You are attracted to the earthy, reliable manliness of your solid **Bull babe.** He can teach you to relax your grip. He is slow to make up his mind and, frankly, you are a CHALLENGE to him. He likes this.

A male Bull is **persistent** and direct. He'll tell you straight out he digs you. Few things intimidate him. Since he tends to be **good-looking,** this adds to his confidence. He is not the kind of guy you have to encourage.

This is where your flirty and feminine side works well. **He's not too verbal.** You can coax him out of his monosyllabic conversation. You may think he's sulking when he's really deep in thought.

He senses how many others are interested in you. If he does go after you, it's not to prove anything. He just wants you. Period.

Astro Alert

His plodding ways could get on your nerves. There's no way on earth that he can keep up with you. You could make him feel stupid and slow and not even realize you're doing it.

MY TAROT CARD
The Fool

IMAGE:

A blissful traveler looks skyward, nearing the edge of a cliff, gingerly holding a white rose. A knapsack is perched on his shoulder, a puppy at his feet.

MEANING:

The Fool is the tarot's wild card. The Fool doesn't sweat the small stuff. Falling never enters his mind, only flying. Carefree, he's not sure where he's going but he trusts his path and loves being on the go. The Fool urges you to explore the world with confidence. The Fool says it's okay to ask questions—to make mistakes. Your most embarrassing moments could turn into the ones you learn the most from.

STAR SIBS

Cher 5-20
Naomi Campbell 5-22
Jewel 5-23
Drew Carey 5-23
Bob Dylan 5-24
Mike Meyers 5-25
Anne Heche 5-25
Lauryn Hill 5-25
Lenny Kravitz 5-26
Joseph Feinnes 5-27
Melissa Etheridge 5-29
Annette Bening 5-29
John F. Kennedy 5-29
Brooke Shields 5-31
Clint Eastwood 5-31
Alanis Morissette 6-1
Marilyn Monroe 6-1
Noah Wyle 6-4
Angelina Jolie 6-4
Mark Wahlberg 6-5

Prince 6-7
Liam Neeson 6-7
Kathy Baker 6-8
Johnny Depp 6-9
Natalie Portman 6-9
Michael J. Fox 6-9
Leelee Sobiesky 6-10
Judy Garland 6-10
Elizabeth Hurley 6-10
Anne Frank 6-12
William Butler Yeats 6-13
Steffi Graf 6-14
Boy George 6-14
Courtney Cox 6-15
Ice Cube 6-15
Helen Hunt 6-15
Joyce Carol Oates 6-16
Tupac Shakur 6-16
Venus Williams 6-17
Nicole Kidman 6-20

COSMIC ADVANTAGES

Adaptable Easygoing Lighthearted Social

Observant

Articulate Fashion-conscious Sophisticated

Aware Flexible

Flirty Perceptive Intelligent

Fun-loving

Carefree Selective

Clever Informed Sharp Verbal

Versatile

Curious

Witty

COSMIC CHALLENGES

Devious

Attention-seeking High-strung

Nervous

Distrustful

Cagey Hypocritical

Elusive Interfering Trickster

Cunning

Fickle Intrusive Nosy Restless

Gossipy Irritable Shifty

Deceitful Low attention span Unfocused

SIGNS OF SUMMER

CANCER, LEO, AND VIRGO

THE SUMMER SPIRIT

SUMMER IS WHEN DAY-
LIGHT RULES AND THE POWER OF
THE SUN OVERTAKES THE DARKNESS.
It is a time when you can **hang out, chill out,** and
put all those yucky responsibilities on the back burner.

Summer is **all about fun.** It's about the thrill of a new
romance, meeting new people, traveling, and a change of routine. It's
when you can create a new identity and be anybody you want with
people you may never see after Labor Day.

Summer holds the **promise of adventure.** Of lib-
eration and new experiences. Summertime translates into fun and
unhurried beach time. Into those breathtaking, beachy summer
flings. Swimming under the stars. Serious sunsets.

Summer is when you release last term's stress. You summer signs are programmed for fun, which is why your attitude is usually great. You're too busy living life to waste energy on living in the past. You **live for the dare** of doing anything new. The excitement that comes from pushing the envelope. Summer spirit is also about **unstructured time.** Of having that essential downtime to think things through without outside pressure. Of chance meetings.

The **promise of Summer** provides a sense of freedom. Of learning from the past and doing things differently in the present. You have an almost **childlike faith.** You believe things will somehow, some way, work out, no matter how dark it seems before the dawn.

You three Summer signs exude a sense of **hope** and generate a warmth of spirit. Unfailing optimism seeps from your soul. Everyone wants to be around you.

Cancer, Leo, and Virgo embody this unique summer spirit. You Summer signs are **doers.** Achievers. Catalysts. You see what's there and consider how to make it better.

Cancerians nurture what already exists and restructures from the inside out. Leos project their **commanding** personality onto something and make it their own. Virgos analyze what's there and improve upon the old method of doing things.

Unlike your predecessor, the signs of Spring, who create for the sake of creating, you're more realistic and don't delude yourself. You forge ahead with an **invincible spirit,** but don't carry along any dead weight. You see somebody's motivations as if they were written on a Post-it stuck to their forehead. You'll give someone a chance, maybe three, but after that, it's ***"Ciao, bella!"***

On the flip side, when somebody goes out of their way for you, it touches your heart and soul in such a profound way that you will always be there for them. You know how to be a friend, and show up for somebody no matter how inconvenient it may seem.

Sure, you **daydream,** but you pursue those dreams and figure out how to make them real. You come off so genuine and heartfelt that people can't help but want to root for you to win.

The other great thing about being born a Summer sign is your ability to **balance** work with play. The thought of hard work does not scare you, but you know when to take a break.

You understand yourself well enough to know that you need a constant infusion of **entertainment.** You also know how to take care of your romantic needs. You plan worktime around playtime. And boy, do you know how to have fun!

You are not the type of person to sit around waiting for the phone to ring. By Tuesday, Wednesday at the latest, you've got your weekend planned. You know how to find out where the good parties are. You love to entertain.

You have a soft spot for those less outgoing or popular than you. And not in a conceited way, either. Your **sensitivity** toward others is off the Richter scale. Your dazzling personality attracts plenty of friends. But you are picky.

You can walk into any situation and know if there's anything in that scenario worth your time and energy. You sense that you are on a timetable and have very little of it to waste with the wrong person, place, or thing. You're a **real quick study.**

You need people. Family, friends, children, and coworkers are very important to you. You trust that the people around you add to your life. Another person's experience fascinates you.

You will try anything once just to say you tried it, did it, and probably blew the competition **out of the water** with so-called "beginner's luck."

CANCER
JUNE 21 – JULY 22

RULING PLANET: the moon

SYMBOL: the crab

QUALITY: cardinal

ELEMENT: water

SEASON: summer

COLORS: ivory, silver, and mocha

POWER STONES: pearls, moonstone

BODY: stomach and breasts

FLOWERS: gardenia, petunia, tuberose, larkspur, and jasmine

CITIES: manchester, amsterdam, tokyo, st. louis, and silver spring

COUNTRIES: scotland, holland, and the canary islands

VIBRATION: intuitive, moody, and protective

KEY WORDS: i nurture, i am sensitive, and people must earn my trust.

ZODIAC HOUSE: fourth

WHAT AM I LIKE?

You are a proactive, **can-do Cardinal** sign, which begins the Summer Solstice. When it comes to anything, if your heart is in it, there is nothing you cannot do.

Let's explore your Sun sign symbol first because this explains so many aspects of your personality, it just might blow you away. Your symbol is the **Crab.** A crab moves backward, away from danger. It also has a very hard crust and very soft insides. Sound familiar?

We'll delve deeper into the meaning of your **ruling planet,** the Moon, very soon, but it goes without saying that the Moon rules the tides, your emotional and physical cycles—in fact every cycle except your bicycle!

The crab is an **ocean creature** that retreats into the water at the very first sign of danger. The crab knows how to protect itself and so do you.

Astro Advice

Ride out the waves of your mood swings. Don't get pulled under by an emotional riptide.

Your sensors are so strong that just going to a party, walking into homeroom, or any new situation can **overwhelm** you.

Your intuition works overtime. You actually believe you can hear what other people are thinking. No, you are not crazy; you are just **intuitive.**

Your friends are your salvation.

You need a sense of history because you Moon children are so memory-oriented. Having **roots** is crucial for you to feel okay about yourself. In fact, you are so driven to reconnect with past pleasures or revisit a powerful memory, you'll fly all the way across the country to see a long-lost friend.

You are the kind of person who always has a **camera** slung around your neck at get-togethers.

Then, in the privacy of your room, in the mystery of your journal, you'll paste Polaroids or black-and-white art photos someplace special.

When it comes to the **him-thing,** you speed-dial five friends or e-mail twenty friends so you can get everybody's opinion on a **breakup, makeup,** or an exciting new **intrigue.**

The other trait that is sign-specific to you Moon children is your ability to **nurture.** Friendships. Romances. Sibling soul-mating.

When it comes to the Sun sign of Cancer, great things could lie ahead with your financial future. Historically, most **millionaires** and billionaires have Cancer prominent in their chart.

With your own money, your secretive, **self-protective** side never allows you to reveal how much you have. You don't really trust people. You know how to save. Your need for security differs from a Taurus. They define themselves by what they have in hand and what they can show. You define yourself by what you can't

see. Money-saved-for-a-rainy-day type of security.

You love to be surrounded by familiar things. Your walls are probably plastered with hot new heartthrobs and your vanity table is smothered with beautifully framed family photos. When it comes to who you trust friend-wise, you can be **cagey, cunning,** and **sly.** Despite your outgoing personality, you're selective with who you choose as your **real friends,** not just the people you say hello to. In fact, it wouldn't be excessive to say that people have to earn your trust.

Since you are so active and involved with causes that demand your leadership, you'll usually get to see what people are really like **close up.**

MY ASTRO HOUSE

which is at the south point of the horoscope—one of the most crucial and powerful points. It represents that warm feeling when you're safe at home and snuggled in your bed. The fourth house is an Angular house. The Angular houses are strictly reserved for the signs that initiate each season, the other Cardinal signs—Aries, yourself, Libra, and Capricorn.

Traditionally, it has to do with the **maternal,** or mother figure, in your life. The person who nurtures and protects. It represents the concept of the home.

By extension, this relates to the art of cooking. You might hate to cook, but the meaning of this house has to do with nourishment.

Whatever you wind up doing professionally in life, your innate instinct to nurture makes you point out where things are going right as opposed to where things are going wrong.

To use a more modern prototype, consider this as your spiritual processing point. When events overwhelm you, this is the place where you go. That private place inside your soul you go to for answers.

Fourth-house energy is like that long, sudsy bath you take to revive your senses. Where you have the solitude, the space, and the silence to figure things out in your own time with zero distractions.

Having the fourth house as your natural house gives you a strong sense of self because it has to do with building **foundations.** It's almost as if you make nests wherever you go. You never leave a detail out when you begin something new. You create strong relationships, based on shared experience.

HOW DOES MY PLANETARY RULER, THE MOON, AFFECT ME?

AS ALREADY EXPLAINED IN THE INTRODUCTION, the three most powerful elements in a chart are the Sun sign, the Moon sign, and the Rising sign. The Moon is as strong as the Sun, but works differently. Whereas the Sun's power is out there and unmistakable, **lunar forces** are subtler. The Sun is about action. The Moon is about reaction. Everything from sense-memory, to emotions, to the dreaded water retention!

Just as the Moon constantly goes through phases, so too do your feelings. Especially permanent fixtures in your life. Like school. It's always the same, but you're constantly changing how you feel about it.

The Moon is powerful enough to rule the tides of our global oceans, which symbolizes the ebb and the flow of life.

The Moon is so inspiring that it has given birth to more songs, poems, and stories about romance and relationships than anything else. Just like the Moon, you are **poetic, emotional,** and **romantic.**

The Moon gives you an aura of mystery and allure. You never show all your cards, which makes you even more interesting. The Moon affects Cancers more than any other sign.

Cancers need to be around water, even if it's just having a fish tank in your bedroom. Water **calms** you down.

Astro Tip
No matter how bad you think things feel right now, everything cycles out. Everything changes.

MY FAMILY

HAVE YOU EVER FELT THAT YOU DO MORE than your share of **diplomacy** and peacekeeping at home? Do you ever get twisted inside when things at home are unpleasant or nerve-racking?

Well, girl, you're right where you are supposed to be. Based on your solar horoscope, Libra, the **negotiator** and the symbol of justice, sits on the **fourth house** cusp.

Your home could be a **breeding ground** for artistic talent or intellectual development. Your parents foster a creative environment and encourage you to pursue things that bring you **soul satisfaction.** Relationships within the family unit are precious. Your sense of family unity helps you deal with the **outside world.** You never feel alone.

When things at home are tense, you feel **off balance.** If you don't get along with Mom or Dad, or if your family is going through some changes, this may cause a great deal of stress for you.

Astro Insight

You need to feel like your home or bedroom is a sanctuary. You will go out of your way to design your bedroom to reflect your moods.

WHAT SHOULD I BE DOING

BEING A CARDINAL SIGN, YOU DON'T WASTE TIME. Once you set your eyes on a goal, it's just a matter of time before you get what you're going after. Unlike Cardinal Fire sign Aries, your Water-sign status gives you an edge when it comes to understanding how layered things are. You are aware of **hidden motivations** of the people that surround you.

A born leader, you have the added advantage of being someone that people can approach. People reveal their innermost feelings to you because you make them feel safe.

CAREER

THE GOOD NEWS is that you don't have to figure out what you want to do for the rest of your life right now.

As you go through your twenties, it may help to look at potential jobs as a new kind of **"home."** Ask yourself if a potential workplace is an environment that you can **flourish** in or will it be nerve-racking, and make you feel like you're fighting for your life?

It has already been explained how you Moon children are very cautious before you commit to something hook, **line, and sinker.**

Here are a few Cancer-friendly ideas.

Since you are so compassionate, understanding, and **solution-oriented,** anything to do with psychology would be a good fit. Sure, there's additional schooling, but you get paid to hear other people's problems.

Cancers are great with money. You know how to nurture it, invest it, and make it grow. So, anything in the financial field would also be a natural. Maybe you could start out small in the accounting department of an exciting company where there's room to grow. Even if you decide to move on, it would look phenomenal on your résumé.

The **common denominator** in all your talents is how much you care about people. This trait takes you to **miraculous places.** It could lead you to the medical profession or out to Hollywood to manage talent on a daily basis.

No matter what you decide to do, it's a certainty that your intuitive gifts can make other people feel at ease instantly. When someone opens up to you it will translate into personal satisfaction, financial security, and social position.

WITH MY LIFE?

You probably know the direction you want your life go in because your **insights** into yourself are so strong. You're an amazing friend. Other people and their problems fascinate you. And you know how to stay in **"solution mode"** when a problem is presented to you.

STARS TIPS ON FASHION, HEALTH, AND BEAUTY

FOLLOW YOUR MOODS INTO YOUR CLOSET—if it looks good but doesn't feel right, keep looking. You need to feel comfortable. The best colors for you Moon children are tones that reflect the color of the moon, such as silver, pearl, opalescents, lavender, slinky gray, and charcoal.

With your hair, **let it flow.** Nothing that feels constricting will make you happy. Be realistic about the shape of your face and find a cut that frames it.

Your weight **fluctuates** a lot. Have your "other" wardrobe so you don't freak if something feels tight *that day.*

You mirror your environment, so whether you're doing a corporate internship, going to a preppy academy, or attending an **"anything goes"** public school, you Moon children know how to fit in just by checking out what other people are wearing.

You **Water babies** have extra-sensitive skin, so stock up on sunblock if you're extra-outdoorsy and athletic. Fill your backpack with emergency supplies for those days and nights that never seem to end.

Star Challenge

An appropriate astro insight for you lunar girlfriends is to adorn the external and cherish the internal no matter how you feel. Your emotions go through phases, just like the Moon. Get used to it. Try to go with your internal flow, such as weight or skin fluctuations.

Star Solution

Pamper yourself! Stock up on shampoos dripping with herbal logic and a vast array of bath salts, oils, and gels. Or maybe chart your down-in-the-dumps days in your organizer book—you will see a pattern emerge after a few months. This way, you can have a little bit of lead time in hedging off those isolating moody blues.

CUSP KIDZ

GEMINI–CANCER: JUNE 18–22

First of all, it's a good idea to also read the Cusp Kidz section for the last sign of Spring, which is Gemini. The primary difference between being born at the end of Gemini and at the beginning of Cancer is that you are far more tuned in to how other people react to things.

It is an astrological fact that the **power** of the oncoming sign overshadows the energy of the outgoing sign. This is especially true in your case because Cancer is at the beginning of a whole new season.

This is the **Cusp of Bewitchment.** Sure, you still have those quintessential verbal skills that give you the **edge.** This quicksilver part of your mind can be attributed to the "last licks" of Gemini's influence.

If there is someone in your family destined for greatness, it is you. You play the political game brilliantly, before you even know what **political** means. It's simply people skills.

You can assess a situation in a microsecond. Your **blisteringly quick** thinking combined with sensible, sensitive Cancer characteristics makes you an outrageous success. You handle people with superior charm.

CANCER–LEO: JULY 21–25

This is the **Cusp of Accomplishment.** This cusp takes you straight to the top of the so-called heap of sheep.

You go beyond what you ever thought you were capable of doing in your life. This is a special merging of the **"go for it"** Cancer energy and the "can't ignore" Leo Sun sign of the Celebrity, the Star.

Being born on the Cusp of Accomplishment leads to awards, rewards, scholarships, and promotions in whatever your chosen field turns out to be.

It is an absolute **recipe for success** in any endeavor you set your mind to.

COSMIC LOVE MATCHES

CANCER–CANCER MOON RIVER OR MOODY BLUES

If you think you have mood swings, just observe your Moon-child mate. His can be a lot for you to deal with, especially because he hides them.

He doesn't have the **luxury** of examining his feelings so he bottles them up and pushes them down. And then, they start to control him.

Just imagine the courage it takes for him to let on he's **fallen hard** for you when he has so much pressure to look cool at all times. Don't take it personally if he clams up, sulks, or gets cranky. His routine? He's goes deep into his **safe harbor** and feels things out. It may take him a couple of days to call you.

When things are good, it's a day at the beach. He's sensitive. He's thoughtful. He's romantic. He'll write mushy poems for you. He'll tell you his secrets.

Like him, you need **time to reflect** before plunging in. You both lead with your heart instead of your head. With emotion instead of logic. As time passes, you peel away strips of your defenses like an onion, getting more involved, attached, and comfortable.

He's **heavily influenced** by his surroundings and soaks up energy like a sponge. Sound familiar?

CANCER–LEO WATERPROOF AND FIREPROOF

Aren't you the **lucky girl?** Leo the Lion has set his sights on you. He won't let you out of his sight until he conquers your heart. When a Leo makes up his mind about someone romantically, **he'll do anything** to win you over.

He may be one of the few signs who can melt your Moon-child defenses. One of his **famous looks** and you're his. His smooth talk butters you up. He makes you feel like you're the only one. He shows you off.

But he **loves the ladies,** so don't get hurt if you discover he has a significant list of potential girlfriends.

Enjoy your time together. It's hard not to. He's big with those **"grand gestures"** and makes the relationship feel more exciting than it probably is when he's not with you. He takes you to the cool clubs and gains access right away, since the bouncers are his buddies. In fact, he always seems

CANCER–VIRGO
SOOTHING ON THE SOUL

This love combo rules! Now it may not be all fireworks and fantasy, but it could satisfy your **emotional needs.** You're opposite ends of the same season, so it might help you out to get down and dirty with the ABCs of your Virgo guy.

Virgos belong to the most misunderstood sign of the Zodiac because of their "natural" house, which is all that must-do stuff like work, employment, health, and diet.

Do not be fooled by the surface of things. Underneath all that is a fascinating person. Don't you want somebody who takes pride in his hygiene, his looks, and the way he dresses? Don't you yearn for somebody who can tell just by looking at you that you had a bad day and will ask you what's wrong? He's an intelligent, analytical, and **methodical** guy who can walk you through your fears.

Depending on where in the Virgo scheme of things his birthday falls will tell you a lot about how he's going to treat you . . . and treat you he will!

If he's closer to Leo, then there will be fireworks and fantasy-filled days and nights.

And if he's closer to the Libra cusp, it may be a little tough on you to have **Mr. Gorgeous** at your beck and call, 24/7.

If you really dig this guy, use all your wondrous watery powers of intuition and instinct. It's not about who makes the first move with him. You'll probably do that after you know he's got his eye on you.

He may not be the most sexual guy on the planet, but this will give you plenty of chill time to allow this bond to grow and evolve into what it's supposed to be.

to know somebody, somewhere that it counts. He really knows how to work it.

You're neighboring signs, so you probably share "personal planets" that make things go smoothly.

When it comes to his reputation, you may want to do a little **fact-finding** to avoid any unpleasant surprises.

You dig him but you don't trust him 100 percent. What's a girl to do? In your case, play it cool. Don't play games, but don't be so available. Wait a bit to call him back. But be nice. He may just be going through a phase of his own.

CANCER–LIBRA SPELLBOUND

It is easy to fall hard and fast for a **gorgeous Libra guy.** Sure, all the other perfect astro matchup info out there will tell you not to waste your time with a Libra, but if he's already in your life, then you gotta trust your instincts.

Go after the things that are available to you—especially in the romance zone! What do you two have in common? Your astrological quality, which is Cardinal. You're both **go-getters** who initiate things.

The main difference is that he's **Air** and you're **Water.** You are led by your emotions while he thinks things out in a more intellectual way. This elemental difference between you could become a **win-win** situation: he teaches you to think things through while you offer up the emotional side of things.

See, the cool thing about you **Moon children** is that despite the tidal waves of emotions that bubble beneath your surface, you have this ability to not give anything away. So, your Libra might actually think you should sit beside him in his **ivory tower** of the intellect.

If things become serious, that is another matter entirely. It would be unhealthy for you not to open up about the things that bother you.

The **key** to having a relationship with a Libra is knowing how to talk to him. He loves the idea of bonding. So why not you?

The only **downside** to a Libra? He can be indecisive, questioning his own ideas and decisions.

CANCER–SCORPIO TIDAL WAVES OF WONDER

Boy, have you met your match! You are both Water signs, extremely passionate, and tend to internalize feelings that **over-power** you.

You're an enterprising Cardinal Summer sign while your sexy Scorpio is a Fixed Fall sign. Your energy is **light, sunny,** and **upbeat.** If you make a mistake, you don't dwell on it for days. A Scorpio will.

If there is any word that describes a Scorpio perfectly, it is **intense.** Scorpios come on strong, exuding danger, intention, and direction. They always seem to be on an important mission. Not one Scorpio walking the face of the Earth takes anything lightly. They always find **meaning** in things.

Most Scorpio guys are **hot.** They know what they want and will do what it takes to get it. They are self-directed. Their lives are always a profound experience for them.

If you are in a relationship with a Scorpio, put on your

CANCER–SAGITTARIUS
HOMEBODY MEETS GLOBE-TROTTER

The Archer is great target practice in the game of love. This isn't to say this combo can't work, but he's hard to pin down. He loves to tease and keep things light. After sparring with him, you'll be less self-conscious about making a mistake. He makes you do courageous things. He's a real challenge.

Let's get into his head. Sagittarius is a Mutable Fire sign and the last sign before Winter. It seems impossible that an active, emotional Water sign could ever mesh with this fiery and elusive world traveler. Since he is a born philosopher, anybody who crosses his path intrigues him.

An **adventurer,** he's always on some quest . . . he might not know where he's going, but he's going just the same.

He's also very lucky, leading a **charmed** life. You know, the one-star quarterback, best family in town. The cutest guy around.

When you are in his presence, face it—you turn into a **jellyfish!** If you are gaga over this guy, play it smart.

First off, don't drop everything just because he turns his attention in your direction. **Do not** drop your girl-friends, no matter what!

He drips with charm hot enough to cause a five-alarm fire. But he gets restless if he has to sit still with anybody or anything too long.

This is **why, when,** and **where** you have to be strong. Continue on your merry way, leading your life. Play the oldest game in the book: hard to get. Translation? Not waiting by your cell phone, beeper, or e-mail for him!

No matter how it turns out, he's a great friend to have and always up for something fun.

protec-tive Cancer shell before giving your heart away. This could be a romance to end all romances.

You think you get tongue-tied? Your Scorpio crush would find it easier to fly to Pluto than reveal what he is feeling. But once you two get all that small talk out of the way, you can develop an extremely powerful relationship.

Astro Insight

A Scorpio in infatuation mode acts remarkably mature and poised. The thing to watch out for? If you two are exclusive, he could become irrational and jealous if somebody even looks at you. If you feel he's worth it, talk to him. Explain that on one level his jealousy is flattering but on another, he needs to have faith. If he cannot trust you, leave him in the dust.

CANCER–CAPRICORN
MYSTERIOUS MIND MELDING

So you have this thing with your solar opposite, what are you going to do about it?

See, the **cool thing** about you two is that deep down, you are very much the same. You're both Cardinal signs who **get things going.** The main difference is your sense of time and immediacy. You also have very different ways of going about getting what you want.

Not to be blunt or anything, but you Moon children can be very manipulative—which is not necessarily a bad trait. You **test the waters.** You can size somebody up in less than sixty seconds.

You already know you have a tough exterior with mushy, gushy insides. Well, your Cap is truly a man of mystery.

He is ambitious. Patient. He has a tough exterior as well, but he can be a **real pushover** if you know how to baby him.

It's very hard for him to tell you what's really going on inside. Finding his quirks is like a deep-sea diving adventure. See, he will never tell you what he really wants. Figuring him out can be a guessing game: if anyone can handle it, you can.

Let's see why. Incredible instincts. You can almost "read" a person. Despite your age, this relationship can go the distance.

You need space. He needs space. He gets cranky. You get crabby.

But your **Cap guy** will never stop his climb up the mountaintop. He is bound to become a terrific success. And so will you. You two can be the original Power Couple.

CANCER–AQUARIUS
AN UNCANNY AFFAIR

He's aloof, charming, and **unpredictable**. Now you see him, now you don't.

But for right now he's got your **attention** and of course you want his. You're scared to make the first move because you can't quite tell what he's thinking or even where he's at. This really disturbs you; you need answers in advance.

Even if you're already going out, he can be hard to read. But when he zeros in on you, no feeling in the world can match it.

But then he goes into this **"zone"** where he seems unemotional. Like ice runs through his veins. You're witnessing an Aquarius in action.

On the surface of things, your Sun signs are not supposed to get along. Let's face it, Sun-to-Sun, you two have nothing in common.

You're a **"let's go"** Water sign who builds on what she sees. He's a stubborn intellectual Air sign who ignores what exists and thinks only about what he can bring into being. Because his way is so much better.

You may think an Aquarius is a Water sign because he is called the **Water-Bearer.** The reason Aquarius is called the Water-Bearer is because Aquarians "transmit" information; much the way water rushes down a river or a waterfall.

An Aquarian is really into friendships, group activities, and has this set of fixed ideas about the way things should be.

If you are close to either the Gemini or Leo cusp, then you probably have more in common. If you are a **full-fledged** Cancer, and you still have this heavy-duty thing going on with him, he will consistently puzzle you because his reactions are hard to read.

But, no matter how it ends, you'll have been in the company of a true original who has turned your mind around for good.

CANCER–PISCES
SWEET AND YUMMY

He's your **dreamboat** and you're already planning a cruise, or better yet, a nifty little get away on a yacht . . . well, maybe a kayak. Yes, you are both Water signs and, yes, you are supposed to **"get along"** and you probably do.

He's poetic, imaginative. But he has one foot in this world and the other in outer space while you are far more **reality-based,** practical, and a true achiever. You have a schedule. You show up for your friends and family.

He, on the other hand, can spin a tale so fast about why he bailed, yet again, that you don't know what's hit you.

Some astrologers refer to Pisces as "the spiritual waste bin of the Zodiac" because it encompasses the traits of the preceding eleven signs. When you're with him, you never know what to expect.

He is **all things** to **all people.** Most entertainers born under the sign of Pisces are famous for this chameleonlike quality. The cool thing about a Pisces is that he's not mean, just indecisive and confused.

Unlike you, who has an automatic way of protecting your heart, he's so ethereal, he'll go wherever his dream world takes him. A Pisces could be a good match for you. You just need patience.

If you can't deal with the **magical mystery tour** he's dealing you, there are plenty of other fish in the sea!

Astro Advice

If you like him, be realistic. Stay focused on yourself instead of trying to change him. It's not going to happen.

How to keep him? There is no faster way to get an Aries panting for you than being unavailable and busy. He loves the "hunt." He cannot stand losing. And he really cannot stand the idea of losing or not getting you. You're holding all the cards!

CANCER—ARIES
ADRENALINE BLUSH

There is more to this **unconventional pairing** than meets the eye. You are both Season starters. You both are off and running before the count of 1,2,3 or **ready, set, GO!**

He is irresistible. You are a complete and utter mystery to him.

But there comes a time when you have to get real and stop all the game playing. He's just a little bit naughty, always in the center of things, and loves clever girls.

So, take a breather and just be yourself around him. He will love you even more. He is extremely direct. A force of nature.

He can be brash and brutal. He moves so fast, he probably does not realize when he hurts your feelings.

Some Rams don't care about anything but themselves. He will pick a girl out from the crowd who makes *him* look better. How sad that he is so insecure!

As an **intuitive** Water sign, if you sense that he is not for you, isn't it always better to be the dumper instead of the dumpee? **Your job?** To protect and serve that vital organ called your heart.

CANCER–TAURUS
ROCK STEADY

This bond could be good for both of you. He is **Earth,** you're Water. You nourish him. He grounds you and has the patience to listen. He's Spring, you're Summer. You have personal planets in common as well.

But let's get back to the **good stuff.** You are both passionate and reliable. You make each other feel something beyond words.

In your mind, he has what it takes. You dream about him at night. The male Bull is slow making up his mind, but once he decides to make his move, there's no stopping him. He's the Incredible Hunk of the Zodiac.

If there is that special kind of chemistry between you, nothing you do can scare him off. In fact, he really enjoys taking care of you.

You may think he's a little slow on the uptake, but he is just **processing** things. He is the kind of guy who has to recite what he's going to say before he talks to you. He may even practice in the mirror, checking out which tone of voice or which angle of his face will make you melt.

What he does not know is that you may already have!

Astro Glitch

He's fixed in his ways. Stubborn. It's his way or no way. Unless, of course, he wants you to continue speaking to him. Either you will shock him back to life and get his pulse started, or he will become even more belligerent.

CANCER–GEMINI
BETTER THAN EXPECTED

Believe it or not, this could be a **match made in heaven.** You two are so close together, Zodiac-wise and seasonally, that you could defy all the doomsday dorks by getting along like **two peas in a pod.**

His quicksilver brain entices you. His way of turning a phrase blows your mind. He is a **walking, talking** idea machine. And most Geminis are so full of charm and good looks, you cannot believe your luck. Well, **believe it.**

Don't discount what you add to the equation, either. Since he is an Air sign, you could act like the other side of the relationship coin when it comes to feelings. He likes when you get emotional as long as it's not due to a fight between you two. You remind him to be more **conscientious** and **sensitive.**

He'll always try to see how far he can go. If he is up to no good, you sense it. You may not want to face it because he is such infatuation material, but in the end, you have to look out for number one.

If you can't let go, just be hip to the **emotional expense account** you will have to pay if it doesn't work out.

Astro Hitch

A Gemini of either sex has a hard time settling down or making a commitment. Think about how your Gemini gal-pals are when it comes to making plans. A Gemini guy is usually guilty of that "seeing if something better comes up" syndrome. This can get very old, very fast. It is up to you to set boundaries. Like, three strikes and he's out.

MY TAROT CARD
The Moon

IMAGE:

A yellow orb glows in the night, a pensive face drawn onto the Moon's magnetic surface. A crab crawls from the sea, toward the Moon's magnetic force. A dog and fox wail. A winding path stretches beyond the horizon.

MEANING:

The Moon means memory and emotion. It reflects light, but has no power on its own. When you connect with others, you develop influence. You Moon children use "yin" (female fuel) to get what you want.

A master dynamo, you know how to make the other gal or guy sweat. Be nice!

STAR SIBS

Juliette Lewis 6-21
Prince William 6-21
Carson Daly 6-22
Frances McDormand 6-23
Chris Isaak 6-26
Chris O'Donnell 6-26
Tobey Maguire 6-27
John Cusack 6-28
Kathy Bates 6-28
Monica Potter 6-30
Dan Aykroyd 7-1
Liv Tyler 7-1
Estée Lauder 7-1
Princess Diana 7-1
Tom Cruise 7-3

Ann Landers 7-4
Abigail Van Buren
  (Dear Abby) 7-4
Sylvester Stallone 7-6
Michelle Kwan 7-7
Ringo Starr 7-7
Billy Crudup 7-8
Anjelica Huston 7-9
Courtney Love 7-9
Kristi Yamaguchi 7-12
Harrison Ford 7-13
Forest Whitaker 7-15
Anthony Edwards 7-19
John Leguizamo 7-22
Willem Dafoe 7-22

COSMIC ADVANTAGES

Emotional

Intuitive

Proactive

Affectionate

Competitive

Committed

Romantic

Expressive

Fertile

Nurturing

Creative

Self-directed

Demonstrative

Healing powers

Outgoing

Poised

Sensitive

Dependable

Instinctual

Imaginative

Sensual

Sentimental

Domestic

Sophisticated

COSMIC CHALLENGES

Greedy

Manipulative

Calculating

Guarded

Moody

Possessive

Childish

Hypersensitive

Scheming

Stingy

Needy

Controlling

Self-indulgent

Suspicious

Distrusting

Overcautious

Temperamental

Overprotective

Insatiable

Skeptical

Gloomy

Overwhelmed

Smothering

Wallowing

LEO

JULY 23 – AUGUST 22

RULING PLANET:
the sun

SYMBOL:
the lion

SEASON:
summer

QUALITY:
fixed

ELEMENT:
fire

COLORS:
power red

POWER STONES:
white diamond, ruby

BODY:
heart, upper back, and spine

FLOWERS:
red rose, magnolia

CITIES:
rome, bath, los angeles, chicago, bristol, philadelphia, and madrid

VIBRATION:
powerful and sunny

COUNTRIES:
monaco, italy, romania, and sicily

ZODIAC HOUSE:
fifth

KEY WORDS:
i rule!

WHAT AM I LIKE?

NOBLE, REGAL, MAJESTIC, AND LOYAL, LEO IS THE SIGN OF ROYALTY. Does it surprise you that the Queen Mother of England and her granddaughter Anne are Leos? Or that **America's most famous matriarch** of the ultimate royal family—Jacqueline Kennedy Onassis—was a Leo?

Nor should it come as a surprise to you that oodles of screen and pop divas are born under the sign of Leo. Like Jennifer Lopez. Sandra Bullock. Madonna. Get the drift?

The Lion is the King of the Jungle. So, that makes you the Lioness Princess and future Queen of the urban jungle or the country manor.

You are born at the height of the **Summer heat.** When it comes to personality, you sizzle. You attract attention without trying. You are pure dynamite. There is nothing small about how you handle life, your family, and your friends.

With the game of love, you're out to conquer! And you make it look so easy, too.

Since Leo rules the heart, you make one of the most **reliable** friends in the Zodiac. When you have money, you don't think twice about buying gifts for friends. You are always ready to do somebody a favor.

You are very giving and generous.

It **breaks your heart** to see those less fortunate. You hate cheap people. You live large. You think big. For you, anything is possible. You refuse to believe in defeat. It's just the way you are.

A natural entertainer, you really know how to throw a party. And you love doing it, too. You have **tons** of friends, primarily because you are such a good friend and you hate to be alone. You always have a great plan or scheme. A completely believable reason to get out of the house. **Road trip,** slumber party, camping under the stars, or hitting a concert, it doesn't matter.

You're usually upbeat and optimistic. You know life is to be lived. When you do get down in the dumps, you can be very proud. You never let people see you sweat. You snap out of things fairly quickly because there's **so much living** to be done.

First impressions and appearances are important to you because you always go the **extra distance** with grooming, makeup, and wardrobe.

You cannot understand why or how some of the people in your life (family, friends) can stay "stuck in a rut" of depression or obsession. When somebody you care about goes through the wringer, you have extraordinary compassion. Without making a big deal about it, you will come up with a laundry list of fun things to do. Let's face it— you would expect the same from them.

When it comes to other people stroking your ego, you cannot get enough. Hey, you're the Lioness, tiara and all. You need the extra attention. You adore having your metaphorical fur stroked, combed, and blow-dried to perfection by the top celestial stylist. But praise in your direction is usually well deserved. You work hard and have integrity. You are generous to a fault.

You are the kind of friend who goes out of her way to ensure that your loved ones are okay.

You're a **born head-turner.** People remember you. Who would forget meeting a Princess?

Astro Tip

Your generosity could backfire. In the heat of the moment, you will give the shirt off your back to a friend in need. Expecting immediate appreciation for your generosity is not realistic. Your need for constant acknowledgement will wind up hurting you.

Leo

MY ASTRO HOUSE

THE "NATURAL" HOUSE FOR LEO IS THE FIFTH HOUSE. The fifth house is probably the most exciting house/zone/sector in the Zodiac—especially for your age group.

What does it represent? **Romance.** Creativity. Risk-taking. Children. Fun. Self expression—like acting, singing, or dancing. This is the **house of infatuations.** Of love affairs.

You love kids. You love visiting your cute little cousins and you have the patience to hang with them.

Your spirit is so gentle and real around kids that they can feel it. They cling to you. Later in the career section, the subject of teaching kids will be more fully explored.

There is an internal conflict in connection with the love-infatuation thing. You Lions are tried-and-true-blue. You mean what you say. When you commit, especially with affairs of the heart, you are a one-man woman.

The conflict stems from your susceptibility to praise. And when you fall for somebody, you **fall hard.** Until it gets really serious, you won't let on how deep your feelings run: As a Leo, you do not let your guard down. You think things through very carefully.

Like, what if you were to tell this guy—who may not last—your innermost thoughts and then, it just so happens, *poof!* The infatuation is over and you are embarrassed and feel used, bruised, and very exposed.

HOW DOES MY PLANETARY RULER, THE SUN, AFFECT ME?

AS YOU PROBABLY LEARNED WAY BACK IN ELEMENTARY SCHOOL, not only is the Sun our nearest star, but its heat sustains all life forms, from the tiniest flower to the most important person in your life, next to you, naturally.

The Sun represents **free will.** In your case, the will to succeed on your own terms and the determination to get to your ultimate destination is always at your fingertips.

The Sun bestows a **life-time flow** of lucky breaks and connections that lead directly to career, emotional, and familial harmony.

Having the Sun as your Ruling Planet always gives you an edge over other people. You are luminous. A vital, **vibrant** vibration.

Like the previous Fire sign Aries, the Warrior Princess, you are a heroine by nature and by definition. The difference? You have the patience to wait things out and ensure they come out well.

The Sun gives you leadership abilities. Plus, the Sun equals the ego. Every action you take, every alliance you make, builds on **your sense of self.** Leo—Sun are inseparable energies and deal in the art of self-expression. You are drawn to things demanding pure self-expression. You invest your complete identity with such things as singing, writing, or acting.

Being **Fixed Fire,** you can sustain a high level of enthusiasm for one thing over a long period of time. This is necessary for things requiring both passion and discipline such as competitive sports and the professional arts.

You know how to have fun. To balance work and play. You also meet deadlines head-on. You'll get the job done if you don't run into your gnarly old friend: Procrastination.

Astro Insight

Just as the Sun is a life-sustaining star, so are you! You can sustain others when they go through a difficult patch. You love to play hero.

MY FAMILY

WITH MYSTERIOUS AND PRIVATE SCORPIO hitting your domestic angle, there are probably more than a few family secrets in which you have zero interest broadcasting to the world.

And with good reason. First, there is your **Leo need** to look good at all times. It's not that you're vain, it's that you know the danger of giving the wrong impression.

What transpires in your household is nobody's business but your own. Having Scorpio on this **"processing point"** is not always serious and secretive. It is a vibration of transformation. You could feel strangely safe at home. It's where you **recharge** your battery, meditate, and balance out.

Your family is a powerful force in your life and you will tend to go to either one extreme or the other in terms of your feelings for them. Your ex-hippie-turned-CEO mom or dad could be the coolest person on earth and encourage you to follow your bliss.

They might be somewhat **lenient** with things that your friends' parents are not. Like letting you use the car.

When it comes to the **birds** and the **bees,** they could be beyond cool or really uptight and closemouthed. They will have a tremendous influence on how you feel about this subject for years to come.

With your brothers or sisters, same deal. Extremes.

Usually you will **gravitate** toward one sibling if you are not the only child. Bottom line, there is absolutely nothing trivial or superficial about your family.

WHAT SHOULD I BE DOING

RIGHT NOW, YOU SHOULD BE OUT EXPLORING, trying the wardrobe of the world on for size and seeing what you **absolutely adore.** If you lose interest really fast in a certain subject, don't waste your time.

The typical Lion knows herself extremely well. You are the Zodiac sign of the

CAREER

YOU NEED TO BE IN A POWER POSITION.

You are born to **have it all.** Family, husband, kids, and an awesome career. You have probably already mapped out your life. But there's just a little bit of truth to the saying "the devil fools with the best-laid plans."

Lions love to **oversee** situations. Be the star. Be catered to. To be told just exactly how great your work is. You put your heart into everything you do and it shows.

Career ideas? Make a list of what you see yourself doing and pursue, pursue, pursue! This is why internships were created. Sure, the boss is getting hard labor for free but you receive a priceless glimpse into what your future could be.

Only you know if **college** is your thing, despite what your parents are telling you. You can always go back to school if you opt not to go right away after high school. As a Leo, you need **ammunition** to get what you want. Whether that is experience or education, you are the only one who can tell what is right for you. Just don't get your trademark stage fright and dummy up when talking about your plans and goals with people who want to help.

Astro Advice

Leave room for the unforeseeable. A twist of fate could put you in touch with somebody in the field of your dreams who will change you life forever.

WITH MY LIFE?

Star. Sure, you get **stage fright,** but that's part of the fun. You also know the stuff you are really bad at. Remember, growing up is a process of elimination. You rarely delude yourself.

Leo
121

STARS TIPS ON FASHION, HEALTH, AND BEAUTY

THE COLORS YOU WEAR DETERMINE YOUR FIERY MOODS. You're not scared to be a trendsetter. You know what works and what looks good. You know how to **work it!** Go from gold all the way to scarlet. Royal blue fuels your vibration. People watch what you wear. You wear things that others shy away from.

How to handle that Lion's mane!? Bangs, layers, perms, curls, henna. What about a **mother-daughter** day once a month at the salon? If you can't hang with Mom, then treat yourself to a massage or figure out a de-stress regime on your timetable.

If you expose your hair to harsh light, chlorine, or coloring chemicals, ensure **longevity** by counteracting tress stress with condition ammunition.

Beware of skin products that make you break out. Depending on where you live, you could easily become a slave to your Ruling Planet, the **Sun.** Use self-tanning products or SPF 15 to protect your skin. When it comes down to makeup, your skin reacts well to oil-free bases.

With your **Leo spirit,** you can always get away with a more dramatic look. Red lipsticks, black eyeliner, bold haircuts. They all dazzle the opposite sex.

Astro Fact

You Lionesses do not simply go places, you make an entrance. Clean lines, color-coordinated. Let your garments adorn and drape your figure. A Lioness knows how to put herself together. Whether it's your sexy thigh-high leather boots with that to-die-for black velvet mini-dress or your khakis, sneaks, and the ultimate faded, white button-down . . . you rule!

CUSP KIDZ

CANCER–LEO: JULY 21–25

What a combo! You have all the ingredients to get what you want out of life because the Cancer part of you can feel out any situation, and the Leo part of you has the guts to get the job done. There might be a hint of that Leo stage fright, but when the spotlight is on, you shine. This is the **Cusp of Conviction.**

When it comes to your circle of friends, you do not have those anxiety-producing suspicions or suffocating protective layering of a full-on Cancer.

You love being where the **action** is. And with your blend of Cardinal and Fixed qualities, you get things off the ground and have that **staying power** to see things through to their conclusion.

When it comes to career and crushes, you pursue both as if there were no tomorrow.

You are still sensitive but things roll off your back faster when your hopes and dreams don't work out right away. Your **superlative personality** puts you in demand. And you are not shy at all when it comes to asking for favors. Or networking. You know your self-worth. Your determination is practically superhuman.

LEO–VIRGO: AUGUST 20–24

Aren't you the lucky one! Here we have the star-power of Leo whipped into the sign of perfection, Virgo. This is the **Cusp of Distinction!**

Distinction cuspers have the necessary stamina and attention to detail to take on difficult projects.

With the **combined forces** of Leo and Virgo, you have ambition and excellence rolled into one. You boldly go after what you desire and have the necessary concentration to discipline yourself. Leo enables you to **think big, act big,** and **dream big.** Virgo allows you to perfect, take constructive criticism, and develop a success strategy.

You are a role model. An example. You rework something until you get it right, down to the last detail.

COSMIC LOVE MATCHES

LEO–LEO
ROYAL TREATMENT

How **hot** is **hot?** This same sign combination sizzles. Brimming with splendor, high drama, and royal moves from both sides.

You're a lot alike. You love being in love. Your goals and values are solid. You command respect. Can't get better than that.

When you get along, you reign as Prince and Princess of your own domain. The male Lion **lavishes** love, attention, and gifts he probably can't afford, but he doesn't care. He cannot afford to lose you. It's his way of telling you how much you mean to him.

He keeps you entertained. If he has bucks, watch out! He'll kidnap you and take you away from the stress of the urban jungle or your small-town troubles. He cares. He's demonstrative. He's all show and tell. But he always puts his **heart** and **soul** into everything he does.

Since you're both Fixed signs, you're both very set in your ways. And you both need lots of attention. In fact, it may feel that the world is too small for your gigantic personalities.

But hey, love is a two-way street, and this may not be someone you want to wave good-bye to.

Astro Glitch

If things start to turn sour, try to take the high road. Be the one who gently lets him off the hook. You're both proud, hate to look bad, or give the impression you lost.

LEO–VIRGO
STAR LIGHT, STAR BRIGHT

You're both sunny Summer spirits who are different in attitude and approach, yet there is an unspoken **understanding** between you that cannot be denied.

He's **low-profile** and introspective and lets you shine like a big, brilliant star. He could be a real keeper.

So, here are a few insider tips on your Virgo male of the moment. You **captivate** him without even trying.

He likes looking hip, slick, cool, calm, clean, and collected. He is extremely precise and believes there is an order to things. He feels there's a clear-cut way to do things right, or wrong. There's no in between. He has a system of **dos** and **don'ts** that are rigid and which he follows to a tee. Even if he's a rebel, he does bad things according to a certain code.

You're set in your ways, sure, but you have an expansive view of the world. He could seem a little small-minded for your tastes, unless he has some planets in **dramatic** Leo or dreamy Libra. If you don't like his list, move on. But be nice about it. The savvy Lion never burns a bridge. It's too risky.

Astro Tip

Virgos are misunderstood because, according to astrological lore, their true Ruling Planet, Vulcan (nothing to do with Star Trek), has yet to be discovered. Therefore, they have to share the planet Mercury with Gemini for the time being. Mercury doesn't even begin to scratch the surface of how their cryptic minds work.

LEO–LIBRA
THE COSMIC ENCHILADA

Delightful Diva meets Luscious Libra and, boy, are you two in a for a treat.

Libra is the **"We"** sign, and Libras become the person they're with, soaking up the other's energy.

Imagine your impact on this willing love link! When the impressionable Libra is with you, your larger-than-life persona reminds him of how much life there is to be lived. He **absolutely adores** your blazing, brilliant presence.

Flattery is like oxygen to you and Libras are famous for knowing just how and when to give it out. They're **professionals.**

This is a Libra truth that should be repeated until this book changes color: Libras are in love with the idea of being in love. During their lifetime, they could write a book about their romantic entanglements. His chapter with you would be the **juiciest.** When they're with you, their entire focus is straight into your baby-blues or deep, dark browns. Libra is **The Mirror.**

Translation? On some level—conscious or not—he mirrors what you are going through.

In the long run, this Air–Fire combo has a great success rate. You may run into some personality conflicts because he constantly revises his opinion when he is presented with new information. You see things in **black** and **white,** so his indecision could get on your nerves.

Astro Advice

You love going out and being seen. You have a huge circle of friends. You're both in such demand socially that you could face some serious scheduling conflicts that wind up hurting you, him, or both. Why not pool together your pals and have a party? This way he sees "your side" and vice versa. You can tell a lot about someone from the company they keep.

LEO–SCORPIO
BUILDING A MYSTERY

Most everything out there will try to scare you away from this astrological mixture. Do not let this deter you from Mr. Scorpio.

You usually have "blow you over" karmic chemistry. Just don't hang out in the lab too long, because there's bound to be an **explosion** of massive proportions in your pulse and heartbeat.

You are both Fixed signs, a surefire indicator of physical attraction. You both mean what you say, stick to your guns, and have **powerful** opinions that define your personality and character.

The not-so-good part of being Fixed is that you can be stubborn and unrelenting. Both of you. This type of behavior does not bode well when it involves lip-locking infatuations.

You're up front. What you see is what you get. You're usually performing and always in the spotlight. He's the opposite. He is dark, brooding, and **mysterious.** You could know him an entire year and still feel like you don't have a clue.

This link will teach you more about the **opposite sex** than you ever thought possible. The sexiest thing you can ever do with a guy is to listen. When he sees that, he'll fall hard, if he hasn't already.

By the same token, you can confide in him after he earns your trust. Scorpios are sharp. He always has words of wisdom to set before your royal feet. Use them. He always puts a great deal of thought into everything he does.

Astro Insight

Scorpio is all about transformation and regeneration. He will change the way you look at relationships and bring things out of you that you never knew were inside. Most Scorpio guys come under the category of "still waters run deep." And if you're the object of his affections, he'll surprise you when you least expect it.

LEO–SAGITTARIUS
SKYROCKET TO STARDOM

Ready to have fun and plenty of it? You **Fire-to-Fire** couples should toss a few fire hydrants in your backpacks when you go out because it's going to get hotter than an Arizona day in the peak of summer when you two start to spar.

Some **tips** on your new crush? Don't try to restrict his movements. He may resent you.

Your ruling planets—Sun and Jupiter respectively—truly get along. The Sun sustains life. Jupiter creates benefits and **luck.** Together, your mutual optimism can carry you through some rough times

with hardly a scratch. You **boost** each other's already positive attitudes.

Most Archers recoil when anyone tries to control them. You can be demanding, but you have so much going on, you rarely get clingy or dependent.

If you really pay attention, most guys will tell you everything you need to know about themselves in the first five minutes of conversation. It's never wise to enter into a relationship with the intention of changing anyone. See what's there and figure out if you want him "as is."

Lastly, if he's breaking promises, not showing up, and coming up with whopping excuses that sound ridiculous, he's doing what Archers do best: **exaggerating.**

Lose him, as it will only get worse.

Astro Insight

Your Fixed quality makes you somebody people can count on, but he's Mutable, which makes him flighty and hard to pin down. He barely ever commits. When he gets that faraway look in his eyes, he's not ignoring you. He's probably just thinking about the upcoming game, working his abs, or the meaning of life. Sag is spiritual and a bit of a bubblehead.

LEO–CAPRICORN
SUN AND SATURN

This unusual linkup brings out the best in both of you. This bond can also last a very long time, if you feel the vibrations are right.

You're both **ambitious** and don't quit when you go after your dreams. This creates a foundation of mutual respect, which leads to a **solid** and serious relationship.

He's patient and prides himself in waiting for the right time to make his move—on you. Nothing, but nothing, gets by him.

LEO–AQUARIUS
NO EXPIRATION DATE

Talk about **double trouble!** When you two finally get together, you may feel like you've met your soul mate. That's how fast you two click.

You're lost in his **charisma.** He's charming, elusive, and aloof all at the same time. If you're concerned that you seem insecure about surrendering to the strong pull between you, don't worry. He's scared out of his wits. **Terrified.** When he sees you in that flirty skirt and strappy sandals, he's toast.

Lucky you. An Aquarian male is a thinking kind of guy. He will come up with all sorts of ingenious and inventive ways to get, sustain, and maintain your attention. The Water-Bearer male is a Fixed Air sign who teeters on the edge of genius and could ride the wave of the future in his field. When he sets his **sights** on you, he's given it thought, because he's got so much else going on in his life.

Sure, he can turn on the charm—when it suits his purpose. But he can become very dry and **unemotional** as time goes on. At heart he's a true scientist and there is nothing romantic about research unless he is researching you.

He can make you feel like you found your other half. His superior intellect tones down your passionate and emotional response to the world. He **evens** you out.

He tends to be on the **quiet side,** and expresses his emotions for you through actions. A romantic dinner. A night on the town, getting down, or clubbing it—limo-style. Or the ultimate expression of affections—jewelry to adorn his **Personal Princess.**

The tenth sign is so serious and practical, he may feel awkward with public displays of affection. Saturn is his Ruling Planet, and Saturn rules the principle of "constriction and crystallization." He has a very hard time showing his feelings, which is hard for you to understand.

Your **warm** and **sunny** nature does miracles in thawing out this Winter child from his deep freeze.

LEO–PISCES LOVE, ABOVE AND BEYOND

On a typical day, you Leo ladies live like the Bionic Woman. Enter Pisces. Head in the clouds, stars in his eyes, not taking anything this planet has to offer too seriously.

This is the **very reason** he could be good for you. Learning to chill out and loosen your grip.

You can assist him with **tangible** ways to pursue his interests. His dreamy visions of grandeur might sound great but they dissolve in the light of day. He encourages you to have a little faith. You are so **realistic,** sometimes you don't make room for miracles.

When a Pisces swims into your heart, prepare to take off on a welcome flight from reality. He's so sensitive, *he* could be the one who winds up crying at the movies. Don't make fun of him just because you may appear tougher on the outside.

He really **cares** about your life. Your trials and triumphs. He can be very supportive and understanding. He's not just making conversation when he asks about your classes, your friends, or your fights.

Astro Tip

The Fish can be elusive and confused most of the time. So, you have to ask yourself how much time can you spare. Is he worth the work? Or are there other candidates that have been waiting on the sidelines of your life who are worth checking out?

LEO–ARIES
ULTRA-VIOLET RAYS

This coupling is **supersonic.** A dazzling ray of light. Your Suns form a lucky trine. You're supposed to get along. So, what if you don't? What if you're friends but there's no **chemistry?** Every righteous Aries has tons of friends, so if he's cool and lets you into his circle to have your pick, that could solve the chemistry problem right away.

Then, there's the second scenario where there is chemistry and it's so powerful, it's literally bouncing off the wall. What to do then? **Absolutely** nothing. The relationship will happen on its own because it's supposed to.

Aries is **Fire,** like you. A proactive Cardinal sign, Aries starts things. They speak up and out. He instinctively knows how to handle you. Your Lion's roar doesn't scare him off.

An Aries can be very aggressive and outspoken: not the kind of guy who you want to take to parties. If you think he's worth a second chance, let him know how he's coming across and that you're halfway out the door.

Usually though, this dynamic bond is the kind of **love match** you'll never forget. Together, you create a fire hazard and people stand back so they won't get singed. You dare each other to push your boundaries. To live on the edge. His is an **irresistible,** unpredictable personality that matches yours note for note.

Astro Glitch

An Aries male can be intolerant, impatient, and sometimes very impolite. He just doesn't know how to take other people's feelings into account—unlike you. Sure, he can be fun—but at what price? Your confidence? Your friends? It's never too soon to lose a loser.

LEO–TAURUS CUDDLE-FEST

Despite the potentially hard aspect between your Suns, there are some cool things about this linkup of love. You are both **Fixed** signs with equally set opinions. Now this could be very good if you agree, or not-so-very-good if you happen to disagree.

So, back to your grounded, gorgeous Bull! He likes to know what to expect and, boy, does he get **nervous** when he takes you out on a proper date. The Bull may be deliberate and slow in other areas of his life. When it comes to you, though, he's out of his depth. But the adrenaline, anxiety, and anticipation are what make dating you so much fun. Just the thought that you said **Yes!** shakes him up. See, he's watched you for a while. Bulls never act impulsively. They move very carefully and decisively.

There's usually a **powerful** attraction here. You ooze passion, he emanates sensuality. Together you make an awesome twosome.

If it doesn't go the way you planned—and **girl,** can you plan—chock him up to training material in that tried-and-true dating game of life.

Astro Advice

Before you enter into this relationship, take one extremely important action. Have a heart-to-heart talk about the things in life that are essential to both of you. This way you can avoid uncomfortable situations.

LEO–GEMINI FLIRTY, FAST, AND FUN

When you, **Lioness,** hook up with the Twin, prepare for just about anything. The primary thing to look forward to is **fun, fun, fun!** He is a fast talker, a quicker thinker, and he'll turn your organized life on its head.

His flirtation skills come so naturally that he'll make you **blush** even without a stitch of makeup!

Gemini is a Mutable sign, which makes him unpredictable. This could clash with your Fixed quality. And this means **what?**

You like to know what to expect, right? He, on the other hand, likes surprises. He keeps things light, upbeat, and never serious. Under his **spell,** he allows you to see the benefit of being more flexible and spontaneous.

LEO–CANCER SUN AND MOON

This same season love match is a unique blend of two powerful **luminaries,** the Sun and the Moon. You are the one who shines in this relationship and he's the one who builds the memories.

Even though your personalities are so different, you two could actually turn out to be a perfect match.

You **emote** and express. He senses and reflects. You act on impulse. He reacts on instinct.

In the best set of circumstances, he gives you the emotional green light and makes you feel as though you can do no wrong. He is sensitive and smart. You feel safe with him. He could also have planets in Leo, or you in Cancer, which cements your powerful connection.

His demanding personality matches your own. The difference is that you lay things on the line and tell it like it is. He's more **secretive.** It's like pulling teeth when he gets in his moods. He can make you feel like you did something wrong.

You're **flamboyant Fire,** he's wicked Water. But Water can be the more influential element. It can extinguish your flame.

How exactly does he do this?

He can be cranky, a real drag, and make you **second-guess** your plans. He has this way of making you feel insecure without saying anything. But that kind of thing gets to you for only so long. You may take the time to reconsider, but once you figure out his game, you're gone.

Or, you could get frustrated with his antics and immaturity and simply move on to the next one.

Most likely though, he will hold your attention for a very long time. He **challenges** your Leonine need to pounce and conquer. He's a slippery conquest and constantly eludes your grip. Just when you think you've got him figured out, he stumps you. That's why you put up with him. He qualifies for the dating Olympics.

His tendency to flirt can really hurt. You are a Leo and Leo rules the heart.

Sure, he's cute, even adorable. You must ask yourself that if he does this thing right in front of your eyes, is it worth it? Not for you, proud and fiery Lioness. Take out the trash. Get back to the **land of the living.**

This is Rule #1—Don't ever lose your girlfriends, girlfriend!

MY TAROT CARD
The Sun

IMAGE:

A joyful girl rides bareback on a white stallion. Enormous sunflowers bloom beneath a friendly Sun. A tangerine-colored garment, a royal robe, extends up, billowing beneath a cloudless sky.

MEANING:

Purity. Happiness that things work out, no matter the situation. Warmth and love lie ahead.
The Sun is rich in spirit, material goods, family, friends, and career. The Sun never settles for second best. The Sun knows the best is yet to come.

STAR SIBS

Monica Lewinsky 7-23
Jennifer Lopez 7-24
Matt LeBlanc 7-25
Brad Renfro 7-25
Kevin Spacey 7-26
Sandra Bullock 7-26
Kate Beckinsale 7-26
Jeremy Piven 7-26
Mick Jagger 7-26
Wil Wheaton 7-29
Stephen Dorff 7-29
Hilary Swank 7-30
Lisa Kudrow 7-30
Vivica Fox 7-30
Jean Reno 7-30
Arnold Schwarzenegger 7-30
Dean Cain 7-31
Coolio 8-1
Billy Bob Thorton 8-4
David Duchovny 8-7
Charlize Theron 8-7

Dustin Hoffman 8-8
Melanie Griffith 8-9
Antonio Banderas 8-10
Pete Sampras 8-12
Dominique Swain 8-12
Casey Affleck 8-12
Halle Berry 8-14
Matthew Perry 8-14
Ben Affleck 8-15
Debi Mazar 8-15
Angela Bassett 8-16
Jennifer Tilly 8-16
Madonna 8-16
Sean Penn 8-17
Robert De Niro 8-17
Ed Norton 8-18
Christian Slater 8-18
Kyra Sedgwick 8-19
Tabitha Soren 8-19
John Stamos 8-19
Denis Leary 8-20

COSMIC ADVANTAGES

Loyal

Super-talented

Glamorous

Big-hearted

Multitalented

Powerful

Charitable

Influential

Creative

Optimistic

Dramatic

Prestigious

Popular

Expressive

Sunny

Leader of the pack

Generous

Star material

COSMIC CHALLENGES

Bossy

Grandiose

Conceited

Label-monger

Domineering

Vain

Ostentatious

Drama queen

Extravagant

Overbearing

Proud

Over the top

Flamboyant

Showy

Unyielding

VIRGO

AUGUST 23 – SEPTEMBER 22

RULING PLANET:
mercury

SYMBOL:
the virgin

QUALITY:
mutable

ELEMENT:
earth

SEASON:
summer

COLORS:
earth tones, heather, caramel, gray, and navy blue

POWER STONE:
sardonyx

BODY:
intestinal tract and digestive system

VIBRATION:
precise, picky, analytical

FLOWERS:
all wild flowers, pansy, gerber daisy, anemone

CITIES:
athens, paris, boston, anchorage, and malibu

COUNTRIES:
greece, the west indies, and new zealand

ZODIAC HOUSE:
sixth

KEY WORDS:
i select to protect!

WHAT AM I LIKE?

VIRGO SYMBOLIZES THE HARVEST.

You know, that you-reap-what-you-sow analogy.

Your refined, analytical nature allows you to assimilate experiences as they come. It is not a mistake that Virgo governs the **digestive system**—you digest the experiences and people that come and go through your life. Your critical faculties are so strong that you can easily separate the good from the bad, the toxic from the blissful.

Some of the world's greatest beauties were born under your sign because you are so close to the sign of grace and physical perfection—Libra—that you probably have some of your personal planets in that sign.

Your motivation to appear **perfect** at all times gives you the ability to almost be able to effortlessly put yourself together when necessary. No one will ever know how long you actually spent trying to get to look this way! A girl has to have her secrets.

Try not to be too hard on yourself if you don't get something right at the **get-go.** You Virgos internalize your true feelings most of the time and bottle them up. It is difficult for you to open up, so you may wind up imploding from the pressure!

Virgo is the sign of the purist, the worker bee, and the one who will not quit. Translation: long hours at an internship, studying, or practicing **endless hours** with the team until you get it right. Virgos are flexible but also earthbound.

You are the type of person who has to have everything in its place. **Methods,** techniques, and practicing whatever you are into makes you feel like yourself.

Astro Downside

You obsess over the little things in life. Is your hair perfect? Did you clean up your bedroom? Where is that killer skirt or top in the wilderness of your closet? These tiny things add up and distract or detract from the truly important things in your life.

MY ASTRO HOUSE

THE SIXTH HOUSE IS RULED BY VIRGO.

This house rules health, work, and service. Virgos usually get a bad rap because these things are less than glamorous. But if you think about it, **work** and **health** become the most important things in everybody's life.

Don't you just hate when the adults say over and over again, "If you don't have your health, you have nothing"?

Well, it is a real snore, but it is also true. In fact, all the elements of your natural house are the things that comprise what life is all about.

Think it through for a second. Ever have an internship or a summer gig? Weren't those people you spent the entire day with almost better than a family? And weren't the real **weirdos** at your place of employment substantial material for a good laugh over lunch?

The **good news?** If anyone can juggle work, diet, and consistent workouts, baby, it's you!

It also rules small domestic animals. Chances are, you are a real **"animal person."**

The other fun thing about this being your natural house is that any kind of work doesn't scare you. And when it comes to the health thing, pack your bags because you're going on a health trip. Acupuncture. Herbology. Vitamins. Calorie counting. Discovering all-natural health products for the bath, face, and skin.

Astro Tip

You just may meet some adorable guys on the job, when you're not even looking!

HOW DOES MY PLANETARY RULER, MERCURY, AFFECT ME?

YOU SHARE YOUR RULING PLANET, Mercury, with another Mutable sign, Gemini. The difference? Gemini is an intellectual Air sign. You are a more grounded Earth sign.

Result? The power of **chatty,** smart-alecky, and facile Gemini manifests its power in very different ways. If it interests you, look under the Gemini section and see how Mercury expresses itself through the power of Air.

But back to you **Earth girls!**

Mercury has to do with knowledge, the ability to learn, and absorbing information on a conscious level. Since you are Earth, you tend to be very practical. You are the type of friend who people literally run to when they are completely spun out over family, crushes, or the disaster of the day.

In your calm, methodical, and logical fashion, you ask all the right questions and are more than equipped to put things in perspective.

Where Gemini is glib and chatty, you're a **walking computer.** You file away thousands of bits of useful information on a multitude of subjects, and always have the right answer. You have an incredible memory. You're a master of Trivial Pursuit. You can talk **anyone into anything** because you make so much sense.

You are also a very quick study of human nature. If there's something not quite right about a person, you really know it. You can be your own best friend when confronted with situations that would literally freak most other people out.

Plus, with Mercury on your side combined with your precise Virgo mind, you know what you are good at, and what really isn't your cup of tea. You rule out things and people who can't give back.

Astro Glitch

While you are putting yourself out there, saving the world with your expertise, you could be depriving yourself of the kind of love and attention you so richly deserve. Get a best friend or two whom you can totally rely on through thick and thin. Nobody, but nobody, can be Super Girl or super human all of the time!

MY FAMILY

THE EXPANSIVE, ADVENTUROUS, AND SPIRITUAL SIGN of Sagittarius presides over your fourth house of family. You earthy dolls, so methodical in certain areas of your life, are **almost wild** and extremely philosophical about family matters. And on top of all this, you are incredibly spiritual about your family or extended family unit.

When it comes to family, you will go to the **ends of the Earth** if someone you love and care about needs advice or assistance. And it doesn't matter how old you are, either. You have certainly proved to be reliable, sensible, and intelligent. People trust you.

You can be objective—of course, when it's not about you. You will do everything in your power to make things better and more **manageable** for the people in your life whom you care about.

MOST PEOPLE BORN UNDER THE VIRGO or with the sign of the Virgin prominent in their horoscope tend to be in a service-related business.

As already explained in the section on your astro house, Virgo governs the **area of service.** It's a no-brainer that service sounds like a dull and dreary word, but when you put your intelligence and creativity to work, doors leading to every single kind of business open up wide.

In urban areas there is a tremendous need for skilled professionals in the healing arts because of the stressful environment. Whether it is from the pressure of working, or simply dealing with road rage, most outside influences are enough to drive any sensible man or woman to **pamper** themselves.

The other fields that Virgos excel at are in **science** and **marketing.** Your brain works so fast and you assess people in a microsecond, which lets you create a need and make a sale.

The perfectionist in you always factors into your work. If you are an actress, you will find a method and technique to develop your character. If you're a writer or love books, you can either write yourself or become an editor at a magazine, newspaper, or a book publisher. Don't forget the **inborn investigative reporter** within. You have this gift of pulling things out of people that they wouldn't even tell their best friend. You're that shrewd!

CAREER

Ideas? Masseuse. Skin specialist—you know, those well-paid pros who give facials. Or give pedicures and manicures at an upscale salon where everyone who comes in is fun, glamorous, and tells you their secrets.

Or how about working at or managing a gym, where incidentally, you're bound to meet **amazing guys** who are truly committed to staying fit.

You Virgos love to be on the move. Since you are a **Mutable** sign, it's hard for you to stay in one place for too long. If you do have a gift for writing, why not get paid for it? Just decide what you like to do—cooking, traveling—and then *voilà!* You just may become a **columnist** for a local newspaper, writing about your journeys, adventures, or recipes.

You could also be a terrific publicist. It's an exciting job where you have to pump out bios, interact with all branches of the media and press, and yet always protect the "client."

By the same token, your ability to get straight to the point is an extremely lucrative asset if you decide to become a doctor or a lawyer. It can also hold you in good stead if you want to be a travel agent. You'll get **great deals**, work with exciting people, and use your extensive knowledge about human nature to help future clients go on their dream vacation.

The other mysterious gift of you misunderstood Virgos is your attention to detail and texture, which could help you leap to the **top of the heap** with fashion design and anything to do with fabric. You are a born interior designer. How many times have you sat in a room, a house, or a restaurant and focused only on how you could fix it up?

This kind of talent could also lead you into

$1500

$950

$3,000

Virgo
1 4 3

STARS TIPS ON FASHION, HEALTH, AND BEAUTY

VIRGO IS AN EARTH SIGN, SO THE FOLLOWING ARE A FEW COLORS THAT MAY MATCH THE BEAUTY WITHIN:

olive, rust, bronze, brass, burnished copper, cinnamon, terra-cotta, dark oranges verging near golden brown, pistachio, celery, and soft, buttery pecan.

With clothes, hit the mall or a thrift store with a friend. You always need a **second opinion,** even though you'll probably end up going with your first instinct.

When it comes to your hair, whether it's long, medium, or short, curly or straight, thin or thick, make sure it's healthy. Study the products on the market.

Learn your skin tones before coloring or highlighting, so you harmonize your look. Diet is **critical** to your complexion. The mirror does not lie when it comes to skin, so write down what you ate the day before if you see that your skin freaks out. Masques and mineral soaks regenerate and renew.

Refer to Virgo colors when planning your makeup routine. Bare almost-there foundations keep your skin breathing. **Less is more.**

Only use the works, like liner, shadow, blush, and mascara if you think he's worth the time.

Virgo

144

CUSP KIDZ
LEO–VIRGO: AUGUST 20–24

This cusp is a **winning combination** of many sign-specific talents. Leo gives you a dramatic flair, ambition, and an urgent need to express yourself in a creative way while the trademark Virgo attention to detail and perfectionism allows you to fully develop your talents without glossing over important parts of the process like **practicing, polishing,** and finding a technique that works.

This is still the Cusp of the Distinction. Virgo's humility and modesty help to tone down that sometimes dominating Leo personality. You receive more cooperation with your endeavors because you don't have to always be the boss. Leo rules the heart; Virgo rules the head. You balance yourself out by knowing when to push and knowing when to pull back.

VIRGO–LIBRA: SEPTEMBER 20–24

Your Nickname? Miss Bliss-You-Out! **Why,** you ask? People born on this cusp have extraordinary beauty and **big dreams.** You can usually get what you want because people are so willing to cooperate. You use the power of your looks to further your work, your popularity, and anything that demands the cooperation and recommendation of other people. The **analytical perfection** of your Virgo side merges with the otherworldly beauty of the Libra part of you.

This is the Cusp of Authentic Beauty.

You don't set out to be disruptive. If people fall all over themselves trying to help you, it's their business.

You just seem to get away with things. You have this way with people. You know how to talk yourself into enviable situations and out of **not-so-enviable** ones.

COSMIC LOVE MATCHES

VIRGO–VIRGO
HIT OR BLISS

This love match is an **unexpected** and **unusual** partnership. In fact, you could be more surprised than anyone else to find yourself suddenly in this relationship.

As Virgos, you both have difficulty expressing more than a **surface emotion,** so in a potentially romantic bond, it may feel as if you're in some kind of contest to see who will give in first. Virgos have a hard time charming other Virgos.

This is a linkup that could most likely develop in a common work situation, such as if you two meet while working on a committee, in a study group, or some other activity where you are both giving your **time** and **energies.** This probably won't be one of those exciting, spark-flying, dramatic love affairs, because you may already know each other. It's likely that something more will develop out of a friendship.

You both have quirks that could keep each of you at a distance. He could be as critical of you as you are of him. You could both feel under **scrutiny.**

On the other hand, you two could share strong feelings and value systems that make this a long-lasting and durable bond. You could be of great help to one another as you navigate these difficult years. You could become terrific **allies.** You rely on each other's advice exclusively.

If he just doesn't match up to your unbelievably high standards— which, by the way, are not such bad things to have—let him down gently.

VIRGO–SCORPIO
INTEGRITY AND INTENSITY

No doubt about it, if you can handle the **intensity** of a Scorpio male, you can definitely handle anything that comes into your life. A Scorpio will challenge you on every level. He's extremely **high maintenance** and very demanding.

When he's interested in you, you could feel like you're under surveillance or being probed by the **FBI.** He is fascinated by how you think, what you think, what you feel, and what makes you tick. This could get to you rather quickly. Establish boundaries right away. Be firm. He could easily have the upper hand in the relationship from the start.

VIRGO–LIBRA
THE SMART SET

Take out your romance microscope and apply that Virgo **mile-a-minute-mind** to this crush concoction. Your scrutiny will reveal an underlying sentiment between you two that makes for a successful match.

His sense of fair play and his effortless charm makes you forget all your hesitations and misgivings. You're **putty** in his hands.

Just because he's beautiful doesn't mean he's dumb. Air signs are intellectual and you may find yourselves wrapped up in long conversations.

The **romance factor** is high since he brings out a side of you that is shy, modest, yet frankly, a little love starved. See, you Virgos are not great at knowing how to satisfy your own romantic needs. You shy away from grabbing what is rightfully yours.

A Libra is the sign of physical perfection and even if he doesn't have model-perfect looks, he certainly meets your standards.

It doesn't have to be so **one-sided.** Depending on how close your birthday is to Libra or Leo, or his is to Virgo or Scorpio,

Astro Glitch

He knows he's fine. He could stare deep into your eyes just to see his reflection. So, how fast can you ditch this narcissist?

Astro Alert

There are some scary Scorpios out there, so trust your instincts. His mouth may be moving, but he's thinking something entirely different, and you feel it. Sure, he's way sexy, seductive, and all of that, but ask yourself if it's worth the emotional price that you will have to pay later.

The **personal charisma** of a Scorpio is legendary. The sheer force of his personality could overshadow your more low-key manner. He likes when someone "takes on his case" and tones him down. He secretly looks for that. You may just have to give him a dose of your **earthy realism.** Despite his secretive ways, he can be honest, true, and match your integrity.

When he sets his sights on you, he can be cunning. He'll get to homeroom early to make sure he sits next to you. He'll find out which parties you're going to. This kind of attention is very flattering. He could also penetrate your surface in a way no one else can. He catches you **unaware.** There's no possible way you can get one over on him. He's too sharp.

VIRGO–SAGITTARIUS A WILD CARD

This promises to be a **fantastic** journey. You may have very different ways of dealing with the world, but your differences could be the very thing that pulls you together.

Star tips on the Archer? He's **spiritual.** An athlete at heart. The Sag rules the thighs, which is why he loves the outdoors, playing sports. His Ruling Planet, Jupiter, makes him lucky. He found you, right?

He seeks new territories and needs plenty of room to move. He loves to party. He gets **inspired** over the smallest things. Unlike yourself, he does not put things into categories.

He's not a perfectionist like you. But opposites attract. There is no earthly reason for you to change anything about yourself just for him.

Relax, hang out, and get to know him. You will probably assess him in less than sixty seconds. Then, you will know exactly what to do.

A Sagittarius is always on the go, always friendly, and **impossible** to stay mad at for very long because he's just too much fun. He understands where you're coming from. You have to give a guy credit for that kind of stuff.

Most guys won't open up because they're afraid of looking weak. He doesn't care what anybody thinks. It's kind of cool. **Admit it.**

Astro Alert

Some Sagittarians are very domineering. They seem to have this mega-ego just bursting to come out. Historically, many dictators have been born under the sign of Sagittarius. Be forewarned, If the bully in him emerges, flee the scene.

VIRGO–CAPRICORN
HIGHER POWER

Welcome to your first trine, that 120-degree aspect designed to bring harmony and a happily ever after.

You're both **solid Earth**, but a Capricorn can be difficult, to put it mildly. A Capricorn has an impenetrable surface that could make you think he's not interested or involved.

Isn't it just supposed to flow? It can. You simply have to know the **secrets for success** with the Sea-goat.

It's hard for him to trust people. He is very ambitious, career-driven, and has this great karmic blessing of getting younger as he ages. Saturn makes him serious most of the time, but he has this really off-base sense of humor that can startle you. It's his finest feature.

All a Cap wants is a **little bit of love,** friendship, and tenderness. He is a **loner** by nature and may feel more than

VIRGO–AQUARIUS
COSMIC CONNECTION

In terms of Cosmic Compatibility, it is blatantly apparent that this unusual mix works better than almost any combo in the Zodiac.

The **success** of this mixture probably stems from your equally clever perceptions. Mercury is the "lower" (not lesser) vibration of Uranus. You are almost **telepathic.** Regardless of the reason, this could prove to be a long-lasting, satisfying taste of paradise.

You are both **cerebral.** His thinking is electric; yours is out of the ordinary. The Aquarian male can relate to just about anything. You can figure out just about anything. The two of you **truly** experience a meeting of the minds.

He is mysterious, brilliant, and extremely verbal. Like you. You need space and so does he. And for some strange reason, you just seem to get each other. You match each other in almost every single way.

You feel like you can tell each other anything. Even if he is part of the current "nerd herd," so what? He could become the next Bill Gates. He could invent the cure for some important disease. You just never know with an Aquarius.

No matter how **"out there"** his aspiration may seem right now, give him a few years and he'll probably do it. Aquarians truly march to the beat of their own drummer.

In most Cosmic Compatibility sections throughout the book, there is a warning, an *astro tip*, and an escape hatch. This astrologer has yet to see a Virgo–Aquarius combo fail.

Go for it!

awkward when you approach him. But, deep down, he is doing **cartwheels.** He can't believe someone has actually taken an interest in him. That is how down he can get on himself.

Capricorns **love to work.** They always need a plan. He'll work for your attention and affection, but he'll expect your loyalty in return. Romance is a two-way street. Most Capricorns have the traits you look for: reliability, stability, and a sense of reality.

If your **value systems clash,** and his eyes are focused so much on his future that he is ignoring his present, cut your losses and look for somebody who is more emotionally available.

VIRGO–PISCES
A LEAP INTO THE VOID

Pisces is your solar opposite, so in a perfect world you balance each other out. A Pisces is **mystical, psychic,** and emotional, which can be very hard on a guy.

Let's face facts: you ground him. He brings out your sensitive and caring side you rarely let your family see.

You two couldn't be more different— he's confused, you're decisive. He's accepting, you're a critic. You're neat to the point of obsession.

He's sloppy, head in the clouds. He's led by his emotions, while you think your way through the day, always keeping your feelings in check. You don't wear your heart on your sleeve.

Running with him can be like a vacation from yourself. He can make you forget about all your worries. When you're with him, you let go of your inhibitions. He softens your rough edges.

Astro Insight

An Aries can be irresistible one minute, intolerable the next. He tests your patience because he doesn't have any to begin with. An Aries can get cocky and conceited in the blink of an eye, especially if they think they've got you wrapped around their finger. Never let on the extent of your infatuation. It'll go straight to his head.

VIRGO–ARIES
MISSION POSSIBLE

The **swift,** sleek Aries can benefit from your rational and earthy appeal. Unlike you, they don't try to figure out why they like something. They act on their reactions.

So, this is truly a **Mission Possible.** He'll sway you with his lightning charm. He can make you laugh.

The great thing about an Aries guy is that he knows who he is. He knows what he is good at. He is realistic about his plusses and minuses. He has done the math on himself.

A great athlete, his attitude is that he cannot lose. He can get those Virgo endorphins churning to the point where you let down your guard, let him in, and let logic go out the window.

VIRGO–TAURUS
WHO'S HAPPY NOW?

Here we have the last of the harmonious Sun-to-Sun trine aspects. At the beginning, it is usually very good. He's handsome, he's strong. He likes to buy you things, if he can afford it. If he can't afford to get you anything at the moment, he will still figure out a way to please you.

You're both Earth signs, but as you know now, you are a flexible Mutable quality, which could create a few problems because you may start to feel like you are always the one who is giving in, or being the understanding one. When the Fixed Bull believes something, he won't **budge.**

You can talk your brains out, trying to reason with him, and unless he's that atypical Bull, he won't change his mind. These mind wars can be exhausting.

You will **save** yourself plenty of time, stress, and angst if you leave him alone and spend your energies on somebody else. Or live with the fact that what you see is what you get with the Bull. There'll be no sweet **surprises.**

On the upside, you light up his life. You Virgo gals are always natural, always real, and always try to tell the truth.

Your earthy personalities will build something solid. Even though he can be a grouch sometimes, you can always count on him to be there whether you're walking on air or fighting the blues.

VIRGO–GEMINI
BRILLIANT BOND

So much in common! You are both flexible, chameleonlike Mutable signs and "share" the same Ruling Planet, Mercury, also known as the messenger of the gods.

He is so cute; you almost cannot believe your **luck.** Well, he is probably feeling the same way about you. You two have so much to say, you probably talk over each other. A **verbal** guy? How much do you love that?

A Gemini is fun until he stops being fun. His antics could get on your nerves. You may wake up one day and wonder what you ever saw in him. You can go **hot** and cold on him very quickly.

Astro Alert

Go in with your eyes wide open. Geminis are great, but they have that dual Twin thing happening and you never know when the evil Twin is going to emerge. Plus, Geminis are die-hard flirts. Think about your female Gemini friends. You love them, sure, but how many of them have flaked out on you? Your Gemini guy is not that different. In fact when he gets going he can be even worse, which makes you wonder what you've done wrong. The final answer? Nothing. He is just being who he is.

VIRGO–CANCER
IT DOESN'T GET BETTER THAN THIS

Like the Virgo–Aquarius coupling, my personal research has shown that this is a loving, **long,** and **lasting** linkup! Even if you do not go the distance with this particular Cancer, there could be a male Moon child waiting for you in college, or later on.

This Sun-to-Sun aspect creates a great aspect called a "sextile." Sextiles emphasize cooperation. You find each other opportunities.

The Moon child focuses first on protecting himself. This is a very smart characteristic that you can learn a lot from—just watch him in action.

He is **attentive** to your needs,

VIRGO–LEO
SEASONAL STARS

Pow! This linkup will make such an impact on your heart, you will not know what hit you. He is **dazzling**. He is popular. He is the coolest guy at school.

He will skyrocket your soul into the fourth dimension.

You two are born in summer, so you're both "Doers." And you probably share those oh-so-crucial personal planets. He could have planets in Virgo or Cancer, which tone down his dramatic vibe. And you could have planets in Leo or Libra that lift you out of the safety net of your **shy-girl shell** and soften the critic within.

He's a born winner and might lessen your tendency to worry about anything except when the romance will end.

He could come on **fast** and **strong,** and pressure you before you're ready. But the force of his personality could make you forget about all of your misgivings and evaporate all the reasons you have for holding back.

If you really believe in your **innermost** soul that he's the one for you, make it last as long as you can. Like your favorite dessert.

Astro Advice

Pace yourself. If you find yourself too far off your comfort zone, pull back. The Lion needs taming. Set boundaries. You can control the speed of the relationship more than you think. The faster it starts, the sooner it will fizzle out.

sensitive, even sensational! He is very **romantic** and he remembers every little thing about you. Like your birthday, and what you look best in (and he's not afraid to tell you).

Bottom line, a male Moon child is a real **keeper.** Just remember it doesn't necessarily have to be this one that you keep.

MY TAROT CARD
The High Priestess

IMAGE:

She is flanked by black-and-white columns that symbolize right and wrong, good and evil. She holds the Torah, yet wears a cross. A crescent moon lies at her feet. She has a Mona Lisa smile and a thousand-mile stare.

MEANING:

Yin–yang. The mysteries of the universe. Universal intelligence. Like Virgo, the most misunderstood sign of the Zodiac, nobody penetrates her surface. The High Priestess is all instinct and intuition. Your talent in the sciences can be applied to psychology, medicine, and fashion design. Your technique and style are incredible. Explore, investigate, and discriminate. Earthly puzzles make you understand why you were born.

STAR SIBS

Tori Amos 8-22
River Phoenix 8-23
Claudia Schiffer 8-25
Macaulay Culkin 8-26
LeAnn Rimes 8-28
Shania Twain 8-28
Richard Gere 8-29
Michael Jackson 8-29
Me'Shell NdegéOcello 8-29
Cameron Diaz 8-30
Keanu Reeves 9-2
Ione Skye 9-4
Cathy Guisewite 9-5
Rose McGowan 9-5
Jane Curtin 9-6
Swoosie Kurtz 9-6
Julie Kavner 9-7
Devon Sawa 9-7

Jonathan Taylor Thomas 9-8
David Arquette 9-8
Adam Sandler 9-9
Henry Thomas 9-9
Michael Keaton 9-9
Michelle Williams 9-9
Ryan Phillippe 9-10
Harry Connick, Jr. 9-11
Ben Savage 9-13
Fiona Apple 9-13
Faith Ford 9-14
Kimberly Williams 9-14
James Marsden 9-18
Holly Robinson Peete 9-18
Jada Pinkett 9-18
Trisha Yearwood 9-19
Kristen Johnston 9-20
Ricki Lake 9-21

COSMIC ADVANTAGES

Loyal   Questioning   **Realistic**

Investigative   Methodical   Scientific

Analytical

Linguist   **Perfectionist**   Sultry

Concise

Logical   Quick-study   Technical

Hard-working   Precise   **Systematic**

Understanding

Intelligent

Verbal

COSMIC CHALLENGES

Always right   **Fastidious**

Isolating

Critical   Finicky

Judgmental   Perfectionist

Demanding   **Persnickety**

Fussy   **Narrow-minded**

Self-critical

Discontent

Hard-nosed   Opinionated   Unbending

Exacting   **Uncompromising**

Virgo

1 5 6

SIGNS OF FALL

LIBRA, SCORPIO, AND SAGITTARIUS

THE FALL SPIRIT

Change is the keyword to your Fall Spirit. Just like your solar opposite—the Sun Signs of Spring—you are barrier breakers, but in a more **profound** and thoughtful way.

Winter, hibernation, and cold weather are just around the bend. Your Fall Spirit is about looking for love in all the right places (Libra), regeneration of mind, body, and soul (Scorpio), and **investigating** the world around you either through travel or higher learning (Sagittarius).

Fall begins the spiritual part of the Zodiac, taking it to incredible highs and very intense lows. The good news? You bounce back, no matter what. It's like a **comeback gene** is programmed into your DNA.

Whether Libra, Scorpio, or Sagittarius, you act as a celestial agent for change. Libras do it by participating in relationships or volunteering in their community. Scorpios effect change with their passion and intense belief in a person, place, or thing. And armed with super-natural charm and undying enthusiasm, a Sagittarius can convince any-body to do anything.

Possessing the fall spirit lets you take a few steps back and sift out the things that fit. You will always be able to succeed in many different careers; you just have to decide where your love and passion lies when it comes to your work.

You intuitively know how to help others deal with what seem to be insur-mountable problems. You have this way about you that makes a person feel at ease. Your fall spirit infuses you with the knack to transform and reinvent yourself. Whatever you do, no one can possibly forget how you have touched his or her life. You don't even realize that a word, a gesture, or an impromptu pep talk could have changed somebody's life forever—in a good way, naturally! You have that much impact.

You see the big picture. You are in the game of life for the long haul. Your Fall Spirit is so thirsty for experience and knowledge that sometimes you don't look before you leap. You plunge right into the goodies that life offers you and if something is challenging, so much the better.

You truly, sincerely go for what you want with blood, sweat, and tears. Heart and soul. Your Fall Spirit vibration is living life as it comes and pondering the cause-and-effect phenomenon.

LIBRA

SEPTEMBER 23 – OCTOBER 22

RULING PLANET: venus

SYMBOL: the scales of justice, the setting sun

SEASON: fall

QUALITY: cardinal

ELEMENT: air

FLOWERS: ambrosia, hydrangea, and azalea

COLORS: pistachio, fuchsia, raspberry, azure, and mango

BODY: kidneys, lower back, and appendix

POWER STONES: opal, jade, and blue-lace agate

COUNTRIES: austria, burma, canada, japan, and argentina

VIBRATION: magnetic and alluring

CITIES: vienna, lisbon, nottingham, copenhagen, johannesburg, and frankfurt

ZODIAC HOUSE: seventh

KEY WORDS: i beautify, harmonize, and can relate.

WHAT AM I LIKE?

LIBRA STARTS ON THE AUTUMNAL EQUINOX, the first day of fall. Your sign is the **only sign** in the Zodiac represented by an inanimate symbol, the Scales of Justice, as opposed to a mythical creature. You seek harmony at all costs. You play fair.

Misunderstandings disturb you. If things are up in the air, you cannot sleep. A born problem solver, you live for happy endings.

As a friend, you rule. Friends are the **pieces to the puzzle** of your life. You get along with almost anyone, bringing harmony to any situation. Adults love you. Despite your enormous circle of acquaintants, you reserve the special few to be your confidantes.

Friends depend on you for advice, but when it comes to your own problems, confusion reigns! Bummer.

The Zodiac's most **social creature,** you spend practically all your energy on friendships and romantic relationships.

For you, relationships are a full-time job. You work hard to keep up your friendships. You make the effort to stay current with friends, near and far, past and present. You never know when you'll need them.

You're **socially ambitious** and probably the most sophisticated person in your age group. Your people skills are razor sharp. You are almost businesslike about this area of your life. Your secret system of classifying friendships gives you a **sense of control.**

If you become locked into one person, place, or thing, you feel claustrophobic, even depressed. You hate feeling roped in. Conflicts **unglue** you.

You redefine the word "social butterfly." Flitting from one thing to another, from one friend to the next, you are a body in motion, making contacts and connections wherever you go. As the Zodiac's social director, your knack for organizing parties and **matchmaking** is legendary.

You feel alive when you are in vogue and your popularity factor is high. Being around intellectually stimulating people is important.

In love with the concept of love, you change boyfriends faster than other signs change underwear.

The Diva of Dish, you always have the 411 on people you know and those you don't.

Caution! You can lose yourself in the drama of other people's lives in order to escape from your own.

Ouch! My brain hurts! You are your own worst critic and constantly judge yourself. You can replay an event or a conversation for days, cringing at what you said and frustrated you didn't have a niftier comeback.

People-pleasing is your self-declared major.

You always try to read people and figure out what they want.

Even when things are great, you look outside for **validation.** You define who you are through other people's reactions. If somebody even looks at you the wrong way, it can spin you out for days. On the flip side, a kind word or compliment can make you feel good for a month. You're sooo smart, but your reactions can be twisted!

The positive side to this Libra-specific challenge? It leads to soul-searching. Eventually you figure out how to feel okay *no matter what* is happening around you.

You Libras need a daily emotional lube job to stay centered. Feeling good is an inside job.

Pilates, yoga, and meditation can balance you out in a meaningful way.

Astro Insight

Your self-esteem hinges on your prevailing popularity factor. Relationships are a mirror and influence how you feel about yourself. If you're depressed, look at the company you keep. Your state of mind will improve if you surround yourself with positive people.

Cosmic Clue

Forget what you've read about Cardinal sign linkups being doomed. The truth? Your mutual attraction keeps you on your toes, bringing out your best qualities.

You are a Cardinal sign—the third of four signs that start each season. The others? Aries, Cancer, and Capricorn.

Air signs deal with thought, intellect, writing, and communication. You have **the gift of gab** and a flair for writing. Escaping into fiction may be your favorite thing to do. **Clever** and **idea-oriented,** you are opinionated, but rarely malicious.

Your mind never stops and you could wind up overthinking. Sometimes, you're so involved with what everybody else thinks, you forget what you felt in the first place. The committee between your ears is in session **24/7.**

Reality can be too much when things don't go your way and you can't fix what's going on. This is when your internal radar should tell you to take a step back.

Put down your cell phone, turn off your computer, and cut off all communication with the outside world.

Astro Tip

When you get confused, go solo to sort out your thoughts. Answers come when you are quiet. Solitude provides perspective. Result? A renewed Libra, flying into a future of her own design.

LIBRA GOVERNS THE SEVENTH HOUSE.

Traditionally, the seventh house meant only marriage. But today, with all the pivotal relationships you can expect to have, this house definition has been enlarged to become **the House of "We."**

This house "governs" contracts, agreements, and partnerships. **Cooperation** is the seventh-house code.

Mastering the lessons of the seventh house is a lifelong process.

Romance is the substance of fifth-house affairs. But the serious relationships that develop from fifth-house puppy love turns into the subject of seventh-house concerns.

You are born with a desire to **"couple up."** You seek things with a partnership vibration. You don't feel complete unless you are romantically attached. Relationships ground you. You'd rather cling to a bad relationship than face the prospect of becoming suddenly single.

Seventh-house situations are mini contracts involving two parties. A promise to devote time, talent, and services over a period of time. Like dating someone exclusively, committing to a team sport, working on the yearbook, the school play, or directing a film.

When a Libra is in charge of any endeavor, success is likely. You consider people's ideas and create a spirit of teamwork. Relationships are opportunities for growth. Partnerships are serious business to you.

Seventh-house "tests" materialize throughout your life. Every time you work through each situation, the closer you get to finding out who you really are.

HOW DOES MY PLANETARY RULER VENUS, AFFECT ME?

VENUS IS THE FORCE BEHIND ATTRACTION, desire, and beauty. Without Venus, this world would be a grim, bleak, and ugly place.

Venus is the power of attraction.

It is responsible for anything of beauty in this world. For that to-die-for physical perfection on par with the gods.

Venus is responsible for the kind of beauty that has hypnotized artists, writers, and mankind from the beginning of time. With Venus driving your personality, appearances count. So does looking good at all costs. Smart and savvy, you are a style whiz. A standout in any crowd. You know how to make the most of what you've got. You're magnetic.

To you, shopping is a competitive sport. But you can be way too subjective about your looks. So hit the malls with a friend who'll give you an honest opinion. Together, probe the mysteries of makeup and take advantage of cosmetic freebies. Ask experts about skin care, color, and hair so you won't feel so overwhelmed.

Inner and outer beauty gets your attention. The symbol depicting Venus, a circle above a cross, is rich with meaning. Definition? Spirit moving through matter. Goddesslike in all you do and all you think, your Star Assigned Ambassador status brings good things into the world.

You strive for impossible, noble goals: perfection, beauty, and harmony. Through the tantalizing touch of Venus, you manipulate earthly matters and attain these objectives.

MY FAMILY

ACCORDING TO YOUR SOLAR CHART, superserious, karmic Capricorn rules this area of your life. As a result, most Libras take their family scene very **seriously.**

Your parents are probably conservative, responsible people with high-profile or important jobs. In the best of scenarios, this gives you the sense that things are **not random.** That hard work pays off. That you can control the outcome of events and map things out in advance.

If your parents are not happy or not together, you may feel that this is your fault, even though it's not. You put **pressure** on yourself to make things better. You may even try to get them back together.

You could deprive yourself way too young of the fun you need by trying to change the way things are at home. You may be forced into a prematurely responsible role because of circumstances, such as looking after your brothers or sisters.

On the plus side, the **dynamics** at home reinforce skills that promote self-discipline and encourage ambition. This may not be fun right now, but later on, the outside world won't feel so unmanageable.

Free-spirited Sagittarius on your third-house cusp of brothers and sisters gives you a strong spiritual bond with your siblings. You could feel like your destinies are intertwined. Together, you will experience things that transform your perceptions and deepen your relationship. This affectionate bond shapes your personality over time.

WHAT SHOULD I BE DOING WITH MY LIFE?

THE WORLD IS YOUR OYSTER. Few things in life won't benefit from the presence of a Libra. Your only drawback? Thinking that if you are not perfect at something, why try it at all?

You are an **idea** and **people** person who thrives on social interaction. You would make a natural journalist, reviewer, interviewer, or on-air reporter. Many of the world's **greatest writers** are Libras. Their intense sensitivity to the outside world compelled them to regain their **balance** by retreating into the writer's solitary life. Writing gave them control over the uncontrollable.

Whatever you decide on, you do not have to figure out your career path overnight. Try several things on for size. The chances are that you prefer something bursting with social relevance.

Find out what fits your temperament. Focus on the **process,** not the result.

Astro Insight

If you have family pressure to go into a certain field that doesn't interest you, try not to collapse into people-pleaser mode. Doing something out of guilt or obligation isn't good for anyone.

CAREER

AUTHOR. ACTOR. PHOTOGRAPHER. Choreographer. Fashion or interior designer. Musician. Singer. Lyricist.

Whatever your **goal** is, find an outlet that brings you into regular contact with people, demands creativity and intelligence, and needs your **relationship-building** talents.

You make a natural lawyer because you see every side of a situation. You can talk about anything without appearing prejudiced. You are a **born negotiator.** You won arguments at the age of five.

A profession where you handle talent in a constantly changing market that hooks you with its glamor, excitement, and money is up

STAR TIPS ON FASHION, HEALTH, AND BEAUTY

Astro Hint

Check out the Star Sibling section to see what notable Libra natives have done— it just may inspire you!

LIBRA RULES THE KIDNEYS AND THE LOWER BACK. Area-specific exercises found in yoga promote long-term flexibility and maintain internal balance. **Soft pastels** enhance your Venus factor. Baby pink, cerulean, ultramarine, sea foam, and azure work best. Always a style diva, few signs can wear as many different "looks" as Libra. Whether it's workout wear, innocent schoolgirl attire, or those loose, romantic dresses, you manage to **pull off** anything without looking ridiculous.

Since Libra is an Air sign, your skin is probably dry and sensitive. Ditch those heavy foundations, which are all wrong anyway, and use an easy, year-round SPF tinted moisturizer that lets your skin **breathe** and looks like it's barely there.

your alley. Like becoming a modeling, literary, or talent agent.

Most Libras gravitate toward acting. **Developing** character and telling stories comes easy.

Your **sympathetic** nature allows you to practically feel what someone else is going through. Consider social work, counseling, or psychology.

CUSP KIDZ

VIRGO-LIBRA: SEPTEMBER 20–24

This is the Cusp of **Authentic Beauty.** Virgo's earthy practicality blends perfectly with intellectual Libra. Key words? **Pretty** and **smart.** You utilize Virgo's grounded, organized, and sensible approach to your superbusy social endeavors. You're not as indecisive or spacey as a full-on Libra. You keep track, are organized, and are focused. You remember who goes where. Virgo's **precision, perception,** and keen **analytical** abilities combine with Libra's charm and charisma to create a can't-fail personality combo. This cusp produces some of the most successful personalities. You know how to work hard, influence people, and get what you want.

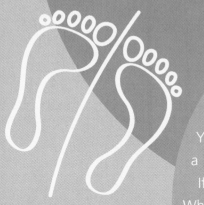

LIBRA-SCORPIO: OCTOBER 21–25

Here we have the **Cusp of Style.** You are intense, emotional, and driven to re-create the wheel. You easily distinguish fact from fiction. You read people in a **New York second.** If you are born on this cusp, your focus is **intense.** When you fixate on something you want, you are unstoppable. You never go about anything half-heartedly. You know how to deal with people and get what you want without coming off as demanding. People want to cooperate.

The Cosmos showers you with gifts that can only be the result of Libra charm and Scorpionic passion. A **dynamite** blend. Use it!

COSMIC LOVE MATCHES

LIBRA–LIBRA
FAN FAIR

Because you are so alike, this will either be romantic bliss or an exercise in futility. Futile *not* because your personalities don't mesh—they do—but because you could bring out each other's **passive** and **self-indulgent** sides.

In this case, you keep expecting the other person to take charge, fast track the relationship, and make all the decisions.

If you think you can be **vain** and indecisive, the male Libra can be even worse. In an argument, you may wind up talking each other to death trying to persuade the other person to see things your way. The crazy thing is that you both get so caught up trying to win the other person over, that you forget why you started fighting in the first place.

When this combo shows **promise,** get ready for **rapture**. You make a striking pair. Teen idols on earth. The fashion police may give you a medal of honor. But your repeated public displays of affection could make your friends sick!

You both deal with life in an unusually **mature** way. You could become so intellectually intertwined that you start believing you've found your soul mate.

The male Libra in love? Adoring. Romantic, all candles, flowers, and starry-eyed gazes. You're all he thinks about. He relies on your judgment almost as much as his own.

If you don't collapse into the relationship, this bond has "power couple" written all over it. **Maintain** your identity. Don't let commitments lapse just because you have each other.

Libra
1 6 9

LIBRA–SCORPIO
NO PRETENSE, JUST WAY INTENSE

Doubts disappear with Mr. Intensity, Mr. Passion, Mr. Cut-to-the-Chase! With a Scorpio you *always* know where you stand. He hates wasting time and he will never waste yours. He's with you because he wants to be. You'll never find a Scorpio asking anyone for advice. His inner voice is too loud.

Since your Sun signs are so close, the odds of sharing those critical **personal planets** that make or break a relationship are high. Libra in his chart softens his edge. Scorpio in yours makes you less breakable.

A Scorpio in your corner is a **good thing** to have. He will go to great lengths to protect you. To respect your wishes. Once all that awkward small talk, which he hates, is out of the way, it's easy to hang, to hit the flicks, or cuddle up on the couch with a

Astro Alert

Scorpio comes on strong. You may have to slow him down. A Scorpio's vibe can scare and thrill you at the same time. If his interest is the last thing you want, try to control the people-pleaser in you because he may never leave you alone.

Astro Glitch

Beware the jealous Scorpion! He can be possessive and controlling. He doesn't get why you need so many friends. Never rearrange your life for somebody else. You don't know when you'll need those girlfriends he wants you to drop.

LIBRA–CAPRICORN
HIP, SLICK, AND SLEEK

So, everything you have read in those magazine 'scopes or astro books tells you to stay away from the male Goat. These mass-media explanations are usually wrong.

You're both **season-starting** Cardinal signs. Your Sun-to-Sun aspect forms a challenging 90-degree aspect called a "square." But isn't it always the challenging people, especially with romance, that teach you the most? He's quiet, **captivating,** and **cryptic.** Just when you thought he didn't know you were alive, he'll blow your mind and ask you out on a date.

You two **complement** one another. He's the loner of the Zodiac, while you're the celestial hostess. You coax him down from his solitary mountaintop into the land of the living. You plug him back into the world.

LIBRA–SAGITTARIUS
PACK BOTH YOUR BAGS, FAST!

Get ready, girl! The Spiritual Archer is a **body in motion,** in search for the next mind-blowing thing. Be prepared for anything when he bungee-jumps into your life.

Always make room for your Archer. Appearing needy or desperate will make him disappear. But this isn't something you have to worry about. Your "in-the-know, on the go" party-girl personality keeps his interest.

Very last-minute, his spontaneity messes with the way you wanted to play things out. He's so hard to resist that you always give in.

Not only are you both **fall spirits,** but your astrological elements go together great. You're Air, he's Fire. You fan his flame! You could also have those great personal planets in common.

He hates phonies, responds to **honesty,** and runs from game playing. If you try to be what you think he wants you to be, you'll lose. If you fight, speak your mind. He loves your convictions!

No matter how long this warrior spirit stays in your life, his influence lasts forever. He opens your mind to things you dared not dream of.

What can he do for you? Plenty. His **ambitions** reawaken yours. With a Capricorn, actions speak volumes. He rarely goes for small talk. He feels ridiculous unless he is talking about something concrete or meaningful. But when he opens up, it's **important**.

He eases your insecurities and wants you to succeed. He **never forgets** a favor and is loyal, noble, and humble. A born **aristocrat.** He treats you with dignity and makes you feel special.

Capricorn men are obsessed with how things look. Their position. About appearing cool at all costs. Having you on his arm means more than you'll know.

He keeps his personal life personal. He's an old soul, needing no validation. With you in his life, he knows he's on track.

LIBRA–AQUARIUS
FAIRY TALES DO COME TRUE

This love match is the first of two possible Air trines. The divine trine can mean **love at first sight.** An instant meeting of the minds. An elemental tour de force!

Here's a real astro brainteaser: Why is an Air sign called the Water Bearer? Air signs are **thinkers.** Like the flow of water, the Water Bearer conducts the transfer of information.

Your "qualities" differ. You're a **spirited** Cardinal sign and he is a conservative Fixed sign. This difference in your astrological qualities should not pose problems because you go out of your way to bring harmony to the situation.

He hates petty people. He is a **big-picture** kind of guy, famous for original thinking and zero interest in staying small. Things slide off his back very fast.

He doesn't need as much space as Sag, but he does need to feel free. You may feel a little lonely at those times when he literally checks out. He's sitting next to you, but he's a million miles away. Wave him back into an orbit!

He can be a provocative, stimulating companion. You two Air signs are rarely at a loss for words when you hang out. Aquarius can change your consciousness about the world.

He may be tough to pin down when it comes to **romance.** His thinking is very unconventional.

Expect the **unexpected.**

A date with him rivals an E-ticket ride at your favorite theme park. Enjoy!

LIBRA–PISCES
TRUE INTRIGUE

When the mystical, magical Fish swims into your life, prepare for a **wild ride** on the ocean of love.

This is an insane-in-the-membrane love match.

Some astrologers call Pisces the "spiritual waste bin of the Zodiac" because Pisces contains elements from the eleven preceding signs. Nebulous Neptune, ruler of Pisces, is considered the higher octave of Venus. Neptune begins where Venus ends. Venus deals with the **essence of romance** in the real world, Neptune deals with the height of romantic myth. The love stories of the gods.

Imagine what you two **Love Detectives** can achieve together! You both live for love. Libra does it out of necessity,

LIBRA—ARIES
YOUR MIRROR IMAGE

Once the Ram crashes into your life, nothing will be the same. Depending on his maturity level, he can be a **delight** or a **disaster,** but he's never dull.

Solar opposites, you balance each other out. You're from Venus, he's from Mars. The classic cosmic combo.

Ruled by the warrior planet Mars, he likes to think he's going to battle when he gets out of bed, playing the part of the hero.

The hero always gets his girl. In this case, it happens to be you!

In no other love match are the feminine (you) and the masculine (him) so perfectly balanced. You **complete** each other.

Always moving, always winning, always the pioneer exploring new territories, this guy gets things done. A slacker is the last thing he is. He lives to **conquer.** Romance is his favorite playing field.

In love, he wants the real deal. A girl who knows who she is. A girl with spunk, wit, and charm. Sound like you?

When the Ram is unhappy, he makes sure that everyone around him is miserable. This, you don't understand.

He may not be worth all those nail-biting, brain-numbing hours of anxiety. Where is the fun?

If he's not giving you enough attention and affection, bite the bullet and ditch him.

Pisces does it to change his reality.

He's Mutable Water, you are Cardinal Air. Despite your differences in attitude and style, this union can lead to the kind of **heart-numbing** moments that change your life. You both have your heads in the clouds, so you can lose track of time.

This bond is not the most stable or grounded. He's a **dreamer,** a poet, and hard to pin down. You're airy, ethereal, and lead with your heart. This may not have the staying power of a more practical linkup, but you'll certainly have the **time of your life.**

Astro Alert

An Aries is short on patience and long on temper. He gets annoyed when people don't "get it" right away. This could stress you out quickly.

LIBRA–TAURUS
THE REAL DEAL

The **Balance** and the **Bull.** You are two contrasting signs that share the same ruling planet, Venus. You both express Venus's power in differing ways but when Cupid's arrows strike, you find that you'll wind up **eye to eye** on many things.

You are an airy beauty. Ethereal, you **practically float.** You flirt, fictionalize, and fantasize. You can be indecisive about things.

Earthy and solid, he says what he means. He won't rush into things before he's ready: He takes his sweet time. And when he is sure about you, he won't keep it a secret. He is stable and grounded. Taurus is the **money sign** with the Midas touch.

When you two have a meeting of the minds, it can restore your **belief** in magic. You speak the secret language of love. The Bull is Fixed Earth; you don't get more **inflexible** than that. Change is not a word in his vocabulary. What you see is what you get. This may weigh you down too much for your liking. Know what you're doing before committing to the Bull. **Go slow** from the get-go. This love link isn't something you can wriggle out of easily.

Astro Alert

The Bull is possessive, territorial, and can be extremely jealous. In his mind, you're a possession. This could freak you out and cause you to drift away.

LIBRA–CANCER
CARDINAL RULES

The good news? You two enjoy **instant chemistry** due to your shared Cardinal sign status. But Cancer is a tricky sign. Proceed at your own risk.

As the relationship guru, you Libras can handle almost anything. Be hip to the quirks of your Cancer crush. If you understand what makes him tick, you'll save time, trouble, and trauma.

A male Moon child is **calculating** and shrewd. He's a creature of habit, hypersensitive, and needs to fit in. He's so sensitive that when he stresses, he gets indigestion.

His secret agenda? To **protect** himself at all costs. He may hesitate to open up to a potential love situation. He's already agonizing about how many things can go wrong before he's even said hello!

He moves **slowly** when he likes someone, making sure it's safe to take the next step. He watches. He observes.

Once contact is made and it's a blatant success, he will treat you like a **princess.**

LIBRA–GEMINI
SWEPT AWAY

This matchup is the second of the two trine aspects between the three Air signs.

The diff? Cardinal meets Mutable. The Mutable function? The **conversion** of one season's energy into the next. The mutable personality is always ready to jump into something new.

Geminis are usually to-die-for adorable. Think Johnny Depp, Mark Wahlberg, Lenny Kravitz—get the picture?

Your biggest problem? Who gets to **talk** first. The Twin, ruled by Mercury, the Zodiac's messenger of the gods, is invested in getting his message across. To him, a word, a phrase, a sentence is a possession.

You understand each other. You're both **social** and **popular.** Your love match could make headlines. And you both love the attention. Together you feel invincible.

Be realistic about your **expectations** of him. Gemini is a mischief-maker, a naughty little boy. He'll see how much he can get away with just for the fun of it. It's hard to stay mad at him; he's too cute! He can talk his way out of anything.

But you Libra girls take the game of love very seriously. If he flakes out, three strikes and he's out!

Astro Glitch

CAUTION! His flirting skills equal yours. You both have a wandering eye and love to romp in infatuation's playground. Noncommittal, just like you, he'll wait until the last minute to make sure he is not missing out on something better.

LIBRA–LEO
WHO IS THE FAIREST OF THEM ALL?

Get ready to be swept off your feet! It's **fairy-tale time** when the Lion roars into your life. His infinite coolness and assertive style makes you feel like royalty. His sassy style makes you swoon. When he zeroes in on you, you feel **immortal** and **invincible.**

You're Air and he's Fixed Fire. Your spirit ignites a steady flame that grows as your relationship develops. This combo can be one of the most **successful** astrological bonds because his loyalty lets you relax and blossom. You want to give him room for those moody blues that plague most other couples. He wants what he wants when he wants it. The Leo is lavish and demonstrative. You want to give him things, especially your **heart.** The Sun rules Leo. Shiny and bright, there's no heart. The Leo never has to work hard to get noticed.

He's usually the hippest, most **popular** guy you know. If he's not into the lame school scene, it's because he's already moved on to something cooler. With a Lion, flattery gets you everywhere. He's proud and destined for big things. He needs your full attention and plenty of stroking. Your verbal gifts do not go unnoticed. He **adores** how clever you are. He rarely plays mind games and lets you know exactly how he feels. He thinks going out with you is a **privilege.** His superhigh standards prevent him from picking anyone who would pull him down. He seeks people who raise the level of his game.

A real good-time guy, he loves to party.

Libra
1 7 6

LIBRA–VIRGO
UNCOMMON SENSATION

Virgo is so close to your Sun that within days of going out you could both feel like kindred spirits. There's a chance you two are **telepathic.** You probably finish each other's sentences.

You're both perfectionists who put tremendous pressure on yourselves.

Around him, you're aware how much you glamorize, **fan-tasize,** and **romanticize.** He motivates you to shed those rose-colored glasses so you can deal. He likes it when you're dreamy-eyed around him, but shows you how to see things for what they are.

Virgo's ruling planet, **Mercury,** governs the workings of the conscious mind.

When he's attracted to somebody, it's hard for him to give in to the feelings because he's so cerebral. He doesn't like to lose control. He's more comfortable establishing a verbal connection before he can even think about getting physical. In fact, with him, the head stimulates the heart, not the other way around.

Virgo words? Finicky, fussy, fastidious, selective, and analytical. Not exactly words to drool by. If he channels these traits into sports, academics, or music, your chances of seeing his earthy side, the best of the rest, are high.

He can **ground** you. Even if the romance fizzles out, he's cool enough to stay in your life as a friend. Honest.

Astro Alert

A Virgo's quirks could be too much for your airy nature. A Virgo's standards are extremely high. Who needs that kind of scrutiny?

MY TAROT CARD
The Lovers

IMAGE:

Naked, naïve, and innocent, the Lovers stand with their arms open. Defenseless, trusting, and free.

They stand in the Garden of Eden, the only two people on planet Earth. They look above at a winged, robed angel.

A serpent is coiled around the apple tree, tongue extended, tempting the goddess.

MEANING:

Adam and Eve. Kate and Leo. Romeo and Juliet. No more feeling left out and lonely. The Lovers give you the power to end isolating ways, to find balance through friendships and relationships. Use experience as a platform for better times. Harmony and personal appeal are in your cosmic cards.

The Lovers encourage you to find your artistic voice. To develop social skills that bring the right people and opportunities into your life. Luxury-loving Venus lights up your spirit.

STAR SIBS

Elizabeth Peña 9-23
Bruce Springsteen 9-23
Will Smith 9-25
Heather Locklear 9-25
Gwyneth Paltrow 9-27
Patrick Muldoon 9-27
Meatloaf 9-27
Mira Sorvino 9-28
Esai Morales 10-1
Anne Rice 10-4
Liev Schreiber 10-4
Rachael Leigh Cook 10-4
Josie Bissett 10-5
Daniel Baldwin 10-5
Guy Pearce 10-5
Toni Braxton 10-7
Matt Damon 10-8
Sigourney Weaver 10-8
John Lennon 10-9

Sean Lennon 10-9
Zachery Ty Bryan 10-9
Luke Perry 10-11
Joan Cusack 10-11
Kelly Preston 10-13
Ralph Lauren 10-14
Usher 10-14
e. e. cummings 10-14
Thomas Dolby 10-14
Evan Hunter 10-15
Tim Robbins 10-16
Kellie Martin 10-16
Eminem 10-17
Jennifer Holliday 10-19
Jon Favreau 10-19
Snoop Doggy Dogg 10-20
Carrie Fisher 10-21
Valeria Golino 10-22
Brian Boitano 10-22

COSMIC ADVANTAGES

Creative
Intelligent
Alluring
Harmonious
Reasonable
Loving
Appealing
Diplomatic
Disciplined
Popular
Romantic
Artistic
Balanced
Fair
Magnetic
Sensuous
Imaginative
Perfectionist
Social
Beautiful
Graceful
Sophisticated
Charming
Stylish

COSMIC CHALLENGES

Follower
Anxious
Perfectionist
Confused
Indecisive
Phony
Uncertain
Couch potato
Pretentious
Vacillating
Nervous
Dillydallying
Procrastinator
Vague
Elitist
Self-absorbed
Vain
People-pleaser
Scatterbrain
Volatile

Libra
180

SCORPIO

RULING PLANET: pluto

SYMBOL: the scorpion

SEASON: fall

QUALITY: fixed

ELEMENT: water

COLORS: burgundy, black, and vampy violet

POWER STONES: topaz, tigereye, pearl, and garnet

BODY: reproductive organs

FLOWERS: chrysanthemum, lily

CITIES: new orleans, milwaukee, and detroit

VIBRATION: intense and secretive

COUNTRIES: morocco, norway, algeria

ZODIAC HOUSE: eighth

KEY WORDS: i transform, i re-create, i reinvent

WHAT AM I LIKE?

YOU COME INTO THIS WORLD WITH MAJOR KARMA.

You feel you have a mission to carry out; you're just not sure what it is. Your strong feelings are nature's way of telling you whether to zoom in or move on.

Guided by a **powerful inner voice,** your insights are remarkable.

Your middle name is intensity. Your emotions overwhelm and, to a great extent, they control you.

Your **inner demons,** also known as fears, seem incredibly real. You're hypersensitive, and take things personally. No one has any idea what you have to deal with just to get out the door.

Loyal to the bone, you'll do anything for a friend. But, if somebody betrays your trust, even once, they're history. You cut people off, just like that, at the mere hint of betrayal. And you never look back.

Profound emotions can **overwhelm you.**

You're a fixed Water sign who can hold a grudge.

You are stubborn and have strong opinions. You believe things about yourself that may not even be true.

Even though you're secretive, you usually show your feelings. If you walk into a party, you think the words "loser" or "insecure" are tattooed on your forehead. If you feel left out, you pout, sulk. You're not exactly shy.

People sense that you **"know things."** You are an old soul in a young body.

Your imposing personality makes you hard to ignore. Your penetrating mind and intuition makes you think like a detective. You connect the dots. You take **control** in practically any situation. You help others handle what seems to them to be insurmountable problems.

Scorpio governs the reproductive organs. You have **sex appeal.** You may not even be aware of how you come across, you're just built that way!

Scorpio's association with **sex** and **death** is metaphorical.

The Zodiac's reanimator, you have a restless, creative spirit that compels you to change and re-create your image on a regular basis.

Scorpio signifies the process of transformation. Scorpio's **transformation theme** is reflected in your symbol. Three images illustrate the three progressively evolved states of a Scorpio: the cunning Scorpion, the regal Eagle, and, the pure, peaceful Dove.

The Scorpion is the lowest manifestation. In this state, you **react.** You go on instinct, not intellect. You manipulate and control people. You always want more and live in fear that there is never enough. You only give if you know you are going to get something in return.

The Scorpion **uses people** to satisfy his own desires, but in your next phase, the eagle gives you wings to fly above desire and use the people around you in a more **meaningful** and **unselfish** way.

The eagle within is a noble vibration commanding respect. A rare bird and the symbol of the United States, the eagle **soars** above the Earth's confusion, flying toward a better world. Pure in purpose, your eagle nature is fearless. In this highly valued state, you intuitively use the talents of the people around you to carry out important tasks.

The eagle **empowers** others, bringing out their best qualities. Most evolved Scorpios remain at this level for their entire life.

The third and final phase is the **dove.** The dove symbolizes peace and love on the highest plane. Few Scorpios attain this level during their lifetime. It is more of an **ideal.** An image to keep in your mind as something to aspire to. Not everybody can be Mother Teresa!

The dove is within you. You can act like the dove in meaningful ways. Like keeping the peace. Saying you're sorry first. Keeping your opinions to yourself. Having faith in your dreams when the odds are against you.

Astro Tip

Make playtime a priority. Release pent-up energy to prevent a meltdown. Stick to a physical routine like jogging at a regular time with a friend. Result? Emotional tidal waves become manageable. Plus, you stay on top of the daily dish, stay in shape, and develop a solid bond in the process.

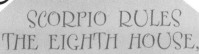

MY ASTRO HOUSE

SCORPIO RULES THE EIGHTH HOUSE, which deals with **sex, death, regeneration,** "other people's resources," and taxes.

Yikes! What a weird assortment of subjects that have nothing to do with your life. Who wants to deal with this stuff yet?

The first thing that will come up for you from that list is sexuality. In astrology, sexuality is seen as a **creative** force. The power to create something from nothing.

Your **aura** draws people in. Face it, you can be a babe-magnet when you want to. You're advanced for your age. This topic can fascinate or freak you out. You always get to the bottom of things and this area is no different. Be selective when getting your information!

That other **eighth-house** stuff? When you join the workforce later on, those very adult things like taxes and finances won't terrify you.

The eighth-house concept of other people's possessions explains your ability to utilize the talent of others. You can walk into almost any situation and make it work to your **advantage.** As a team captain, you know which positions people should play. You know which people can help you when, for example, you audition for the school play or try to find the 411 on that cute new guy in English.

In group situations, you tend to be the leader. People trust you to promote their interests. People tell you things they won't tell anyone else.

Having the eighth house as your natural domain can also mean you may wind up with a nifty **inheritance** during your lifetime.

Astro Advice

If the idea of talking to your parents about the hormonal changes going on in your body flips you out, find someone older who you can trust. Like that "been there, done that" sophisticated relative, or that very cool teacher you admire. They'd be happy to give you the real deal on life and love.

HOW DOES MY PLANETARY RULER, PLUTO, AFFECT ME?

THERE IS NOTHING DULL, BLAH, OR BORING ABOUT YOU. Your ruling planet, Pluto, sees to that. Most astrologers consider Pluto to be the higher vibration of Mars. Where Mars is the soldier on the battlefield, Pluto is the four-star general who makes the rules and calls the shots.

Another cool astrological theory floating around about Pluto is that it was only discovered when the collective unconscious of humankind was ready to understand what **Plutonian energy** meant.

Pluto's discovery in the 1930s coincided with the discovery of the atom and the creation of the atom bomb. This accounts for your explosive energy. Scorpio embodies Pluto's power.

Pluto moves around the Zodiac so slowly that it can stay twenty years in one sign. Considered the generational planet, an entire generation is born while it transits through a single sign. This accounts for the '70s peace-and-love generation. Pluto hung out in Libra, the sign of **peace** and love, for this entire decade.

On a personal level, Plutonian energy bestows willpower, purpose, and a "never say die" attitude. The word *quit* isn't in your vocabulary. You never give up.

Pluto gives you the power to transform pain into pleasure. You can morph an embarrassing moment into awesome lyrics for a hit song. A romantic disaster into a **prizewinning** short story. Use the angst of a season's defeat to summon up the stuff to bring your team to victory in that critical game.

You turn things around when they're headed nowhere but down.

Astro Alert

Pluto's downside? You can be secretive, obsessive, and not know when to stop.

MY FAMILY

ACCORDING TO YOUR SOLAR CHART, electric Aquarius energy influences your domestic life. With the quirky eleventh sign ruling this pivotal point in your 'scope, anything goes.

What a **scene!** Never tedious. Sometimes you need to leave just to chill out.

Your parents could lead unconventional lives. They could act more as friends than authority figures. They could create a **nontraditional** atmosphere at home where the usual rules don't apply. They could be overgrown hipsters who let you do your thing and urge you to follow your dreams.

Kind of takes the rebellion out of you, huh?

They may have multiple marriages which produce a sprawling relative pool, filled with big personalities and a long list of step- and half-siblings.

With erratic Aquarius affecting your home base, sudden relocations could be the norm. You may be **yanked** from one school or community and be forced to adapt to a new one on a regular basis.

Family upheavals give you skills to deal with the real world. External chaos makes you more **solid** internally and fuses the family together. You learn to adjust to new situations in no time.

WHAT SHOULD I BE DOING

AS IF ANYBODY CAN TELL *YOU* WHAT TO DO!

You may take a few detours during your teenage years, but **detours** turn into **destiny.** You know how to turn any setback into an opportunity.

You'd love to make oodles of cash while still doing something socially relevant. You'll try to stay true to your vision if only you can just make your own rules. You're **fueled** with the inspiration to, hey, no big deal, do the impossible.

Today, infinite options exist for the girl who dares to be real. You thrive in situations

CAREER

YOU WILL FIND SCORPIOS IN EVERY LINE OF WORK, in every industry, in every capacity. Of course, you have to start somewhere, but the truth is, most Scorpios rarely stay in the **entry-level** stage for too long.

You need to be your own boss or work unsupervised. Scorpios need a **large playing field.** Nothing daunts you. You like to find a challenge you can really sink your teeth into.

Your detective nature loves a mystery. You could easily see yourself dedicating your life to **research,** academic study, human behavior, or psychology.

The idea of finding a world where you can never reach the end intrigues you. Like trying your luck in the cutthroat world of fashion, big business, entertainment, or the media.

You're the kind of person who'd rather go out and a make a movie on her own than wait around for other people to make decisions. You'll find the funding and the people to help make it happen, but it's your **eagle-eyed** vision that drives it home.

If you coach after competing in a particular sport, you'll find a way to incorporate your experience into a breakthrough teaching method that could change the way the sport is taught.

People **open up to** you. You know how to listen. Therapy or counseling would quench your thirst for understanding what makes people tick.

Working in finance, real estate, or handling literary properties would be in line with your eighth house theme of other people's resources.

WITH MY LIFE?

where you are continually challenged to do increasingly difficult tasks. The more difficult, the better. **Bring it on!**

Anything with mystery, danger, and depth gets your attention. Naturally, you will choose an area requiring that you dig down deep and give 110 percent of your energy in order to reap the rewards.

Nothing is too risky or ambitious. You don't like to play it safe. You need a really big pond.

STAR TIPS ON FASHION, HEALTH, AND BEAUTY

AS AN INTENSE AND SEXY SCORPIO, you are drawn to wearing black, **black,** and **more black.** You could have more than twenty-eight black skirts, thirty-nine black tops, and twelve black jackets and counting. Why not mix it up a bit with lavender, clover, fire-engine red, and ruby?

Your **hair** probably feels like it has a mind of its own. You are always on the lookout for a way to make it do what you want. You can't understand why other people think it's so great.

If you live in the pool, at the gym, or on the field, be smart. Wash out the sea salt, chlorine, toxins, whatever, with a **timesaving** shampoo-detangler-conditioner combo.

Scorpios tend to have combination skin. Your **emotions** show in your skin. Makeup should enhance your appearance, not make bad skin look worse. Foundations are the key to a fabulous face. Use the bare minimum unless the date is worth it. Pay attention to your crucial T-zone and **prevent** zits before they surface.

CUSP KIDZ

LIBRA–SCORPIO: OCTOBER 21–25

You are born on the **Cusp of Conquest.** Know it. Own it.

The universe serves up a cosmic enchilada filled with the necessary personality and physical equipment to win over friends and influence people.

Your charm and beauty can be attributed to the exiting influence of **glam-girl** Venus.

Pluto's power gives you the character of a **leader.** You are the anointed one.

With this bewitching blend of goddess Venus with the born appeal of sexy Pluto, you're cooking with gas!

SCORPIO–SAGITTARIUS: NOVEMBER 19–23

Being born on the **Cusp of Adventure** ensures that your life will be stuffed with enlightening and mind-blowing experiences.

Once you get a taste of being free and on your own, no one can stop your quest, not even *him.*

Even when you are really young, you shrug your shoulders at the thought of being tied down when there's so much in life to explore.

Your seasonal spirit lets you see the **Big Picture.**

Add this to the winning combination of Scorpio's intensity and focus and Sagittarius's global, optimistic attitude, and you're on your way to becoming a **skyrocket** to success.

COSMIC LOVE MATCHES

SCORPIO–SCORPIO
HIP TO HIS TRICKS

Can this same-sign, white-water-rapids of a cosmic combo last past the stroke of midnight with both parties still intact and standing?

Even on a bad day, you are **painfully aware** of yourself and of every nuance of any situation you find yourself in.

He's the same, except he doesn't have the advantage of spilling his guts to a guy friend about you before homeroom. You, the girl, have society's permission to be your **starry-eyed,** mood-swinging emotional self.

He has to act all cool, like he has it all together and knows what he's doing. He goes through all the same painful adolescent stuff as you with absolutely no outlet.

Whether or not you two go the distance, be assured that your mutual **intensity** will change your perspectives and perceptions forever.

For some strange reason even the stars cannot explain, you will never be the same after your love link with a Scorpio male.

He spoils you for anyone else. You may not realize how much he changes the way you feel. He **encourages** you to confront the things that scare you most.

Be yourself, but make him work for every kiss, every secret, and every moment of your time. This way, no matter what happens in the long run, you'll know that even though you wanted to you didn't chase him down.

You'll **always** have the upper hand.

Between Scorpios, this is a critical thing. And he'll always wonder if . . . And he'll always be just a little bit more manageable.

Astro Tip

If you want him, be coy at first. If he knows how you feel, it won't be as fun for him to get you. Keep him guessing, let the games begin. Every inch he gains makes him feel like he has accomplished something.

Astro Tip

Never stop doing the things you love. They're what attracted him to you in the first place. Don't make life something you do between boyfriends.

SCORPIO–SAGITTARIUS
UPBEAT AND UNBEATABLE

You are both in the same season, but approach life very differently. Sharing personal planets will make things much easier on both of you.

A huge **hint?** Sir Jupiter, the cosmic fortune cookie, is his planetary ruler. His luck never seems to run out. Hearing about his nonstop lucky streak could make you wonder what you're doing wrong. His **uplifting** personality makes you feel better just by being in the same room. His "keep it light at all costs" policy does wonders for your tendency to overanalyze and think the worst is about to happen. He'll turn your angst into Easy Street.

The broadminded Sagittarius challenges how you think. It's not that he has a problem with the way you are, he just wants to understand why you fixate on things.

He rarely has a hidden agenda. He takes things as they come. Having a Sag in your life is like skipping school. You are tempted to **drop everything** at a moment's notice, and you probably do, because he always has something much better to do.

Homework can wait. Your friends will understand.

But he can blow out of your life as fast as he blew in. Try not to **bail** out on everything just for him.

Astro Alert

A Sagittarius needs plenty of space. When he gets struck with his signature wanderlust, and he will, don't take it personally when he splits.

SCORPIO–CAPRICORN
SOLID GOLD

If any sign in the Zodiac is equipped to handle the solemn, dark, brooding, and mysterious male Capricorn, baby, it is you.

He has a dry **wit** most others can't even pick up on. You always get the joke. His sense of humor helps you feel someone else besides you has figured out how absurd life on planet Earth can be.

When he's more comfortable with you, he'll show you a side he never lets anyone see. He uses different faces to cope with different situations. When he feels safe with you he'll tell you personal things. **Deep down,** he needs somebody to confide in.

He is loyal, has a good soul, and won't try to fool you just to look cool. He doesn't have to. A Capricorn is ahead of his chronological years. He knows himself.

He singles you out because he knows you can accomplish more as a couple. Stoic, brave, he's a real **keeper.** Stay close.

Unlike some guys who throw up a wall and move onto their next victim after they "get" you in their silly game of Spot, Chase, and Conquer, the Cap is just getting started with you after he says hello.

Astro Insight

The loner of the Zodiac has no time to waste as he climbs to the top of his metaphorical mountain.

SCORPIO–PISCES
SMOOTH SAILING

This combo is the first of two tempting Water trines; the second one for you is **Mr. Moonchild.**

The only possible thing that could mess with this mesmerizing mixture is how your different qualities interact. You are a trusty, Fixed Sign, where he is a mystical Mutable sign. His otherworldly appeal makes him that much more attractive.

Emotionally, you **connect.** Your feelings intertwine. You've both found your soul mate. There can be times when you're too eager and **obsessive** or he's way too dazed and confused. Hard to pin down, he answers to a higher force, invisible to the naked eye. Even when he's by your side, his imagination could be light-years away.

SCORPIO–AQUARIUS
FIXATION RELATION

You're Water, he's Air. Your signs have little in common, which doesn't mean it can't work out. You two are both so complicated that this could keep you two on your toes for months. Your Sun signs form an aspect called a **square.** Even though this can create conflict and a difference of opinion, that knee-knocking, heart-pounding, **electric shock** wave of a reaction is practically never not there. It is this extraordinary chemistry that keeps you coming back for more. Making a fresh start. Making sure that this time you'll both make an effort to change. But you never do. As Fixed signs, you are usually set in your ways before you start kindergarten. Right?

An Aquarian walks to the beat of his own drummer. The more authentic and relaxed you are, the more demonstrative he'll be. The more **mysterious** and impenetrable, the more he likes it. The very thing

that brought you two together can break you apart. Your equally set ways of thinking could work against you after that first flush of **infatuation** fades. As real life penetrates your romantic bubble, you could discover that your values simply don't mesh.

Where you can be intense and passionate, he can be remote and unemotional. In an argument, he can talk circles around you (Air) while your **titanic emotions** (Water) can rip him in two.

The great thing about an Aquarius male is that he is so altruistic he will do everything in his power to part as friends.

A gentle **nudge** from you reminds your space cadet to return to planet Earth.

He does wonders for your creative side. Face it, you can be your own worst critic, predicting disaster before you've even begun something new.

Your self-doubt amazes him. He can make you believe in the most far-fetched idea, since he can imagine anything. He's real **dreamer** and a very cool guy.

SCORPIO–ARIES
DYNAMIC DUO

Before Pluto was discovered, you and the warrior Ram shared **Mars** as a ruling planet. Even though this no longer applies, you still have very similar characteristics.

Deep **emotions,** big personalities, and strong **feelings.**

You take longer to react than he does. You savor your time together, replaying every moment over and over in your mind. He moves fast and furious, rushing in your life like a wild brushfire, **igniting** all your senses at once. You internalize your feelings, while he acts on his.

Pure infatuation material, he is a walking **adrenaline** rush. Irresistible but insensitive, there are plenty of reasons to watch out and protect yourself from being burned.

His **charisma** is strong enough to make you give in to him right away. You may be tempted to let your guard down and collapse into the drama he creates.

Before you can blink, you may find yourself alone. **Exposed.** Just when you thought things were starting, he's already moved on to somebody else.

Astro Insight

Earthy and anchored in reality, he is also the money sign. He's got that "protector" vibe going on way before his peers. He'll wine you, dine you, and always have the best tickets to see your favorite band. He knows how to do all that stuff.

SCORPIO–TAURUS
A MATCH THAT WON'T BLOW OUT

Taurus and Scorpio are solar opposites, so, in a sense, this illustrates the reunion of **two halves.** Each complementing what the other sign lacks.

Get ready for your temperatures to rise. There is serious chemistry here. You are both **sensual** and driven to be in a relationship. He, for sensible reasons. You, for elaborate ones.

He likes to keep things **simple**, which is an excellent thing. Complex and hypersensitive, you can complicate even the simplest thing.

Your fixed qualities make you equally dependable. This love match has a good

SCORPIO–GEMINI
EFFERVESCENT AND IRIDESCENT

You **heavy-handed** Scorpios benefit from the mischievous Gemini, the Zodiac's charmer, skipping across your path. You both learn from this linkup.

He's playful. The Prince of Flirtation. Serious things roll off his back faster than you can say his name. Naturally upbeat, he makes you laugh.

He watches you when you're not looking. Your **"never say die"** attitude impresses him. You fascinate and hypnotize him. He can't figure out how on earth you do what you do. And you do it so well!

Most astro info tells you this combo can't work. But, that's simply wrong, it is a very **constructive** matchup. You just need to work harder because you both come from such different emotional realities.

He makes you lighten up. You make him look beneath the surface of things to find meaning.

A Mutable sign, he's **fluid,** like quicksilver, and very hard to pin down. He has this really cute quality that keeps him eternally young.

chance of working out because of this trait. When you **believe** in something, that's that.

No matter how many petty things happen, you know it would be stupid to let them rock the boat.

Astro Insight

Geminis are so entertaining, you may not realize how much he's changing your attitude because you're laughing so much. You're free from those black moods that hold you hostage. Hanging out with the Twin is like a day at the beach. Just remember to slather on emotional sunblock with SPF 35. He's that dazzling!

Astro Hint

Water equals emotion. Emotions control you both. If you agree to discuss the funky things that arise in a relationship and not let things fester, this could last a long time.

SCORPIO–CANCER
WATER WONDERLAND

This crush-combo with Mr. Moon Child can astonish you. It keeps getting better.

You are both **manipulative** in order to deal with people and pressures of the world. He protects himself at all costs and is on a perpetual quest for security. You, on the other hand, are on a search for power, and you usually get what you want.

Cancer reveals only what's necessary to stay comfortable. Even when the moon is full, you only see one side. But your X-ray eyes see all. You sense the unspoken. He is drawn into your magnetic field.

The Moon Child automatically makes you feel like "taking care" of him. He has a way of selecting someone who satisfies his needs. Your efforts won't go unrewarded. A Cancer is for life.

Sensitive and devoted, he builds on the present so he can have a past. He creates the stuff of memories, and goes out of his way to make your "together time" special. Face facts! You are a power couple.

SCORPIO–LEO
LOVE AND CRUSHABILITY

This never starts out quiet. Never starts small. The universe **isn't subtle** when it sets its sights on getting you two together. You'll literally crash into each other on the road, the field, or in the hall between classes.

It's as if destiny can't wait to watch the fireworks unfold in this roller-coaster ride of a relationship.

But the **Jungle King** needs to be acknowledged for everything he does. This may tick you off, because you hate when people expect you to do something. If it's your idea, cool, but if you feel pressure from an outside force, you **rebel.**

How hard can it be to whisper softly in his ear?

You are both very strong. He's outgoing, demonstrative, and ruled by the Sun. He **craves** the spotlight. He loves to perform. Since your behavior is more guarded, together you could accomplish a lot since you don't compete for attention.

In love, remember he needs adoration and things will go remarkably well. Encore!

SCORPIO–VIRGO
PRACTICAL MAGIC

This love link is **smart** and **practical.** It may not be as wild as some of the others, but it lasts longer. You both want **similar** things and your value systems are compatible.

The main feature of the Water–Earth combo? How you nourish the very businesslike and analytical Virgo.

How he helps you create **boundaries.** He shows you how to pinpoint things when your emotions cloud and confuse.

You both focus on long-term achievement, so there is very little that is frivolous between you. It is very reality based. You two could hook up in a study group or other situation that isn't overtly social or partylike.

You both enjoy working together toward the same **goals,** and we're not talking ice hockey or soccer. We're talking happiness.

During these funky, pimply teenage years, you can support and encourage each other. Meditate on your mutual ruling planets. Transforming Pluto changes everything it touches. When it unites with the chatty Mercury, he'll never think the same again.

Astro Clue

Virgo is eccentric. His mind zooms along at the speed of sound. It's like a computer. When you see him get anxious and tense, tell him to click "Home," put on his cerebral screen saver, and take a chill pill.

SCORPIO–LIBRA
PLANETARY POWER SHOWER

Born in the fall, you probably have those awesome **personal planets** in common. The more you know about your chart, the better when it comes to this combo because you are both high maintenance.

If you know when you were born, look up your **Ascendant** in the introduction to this book. Any additional information will help you assess your compatibility factor with Libra.

You're Water, he's Air. You're both Fall signs with the desire to change how things are.

You take Libra's relationship theme further and deeper. You **challenge** him to go beyond the surface and not be so superficial. You expect the best from him and he will rise to the challenge. The last thing a Libra wants is to disappoint.

He lives for approval, which doesn't necessarily make him wishy-washy. He is on a quest to perfect the relationships he's in. You make him work hard for everything. He shows you how to ease up on yourself.

You both have amazing willpower when it comes down to getting the things that matter most in both of your lives.

Mr. Libra is the **ultimate romantic** and loves to initiate things. He will absolutely alter your reality. A talkative Air sign, he speaks the language of the heart. Go for it, girl!

Astro Clue

The Libra doesn't feel normal if he's unattached. Your passion won't scare him off if he's got planets in Scorpio or you have planets in Libra. Talk about a planetary power shower!

MY TAROT CARD
The Star

IMAGE:

Seven tiny white stars surround an eight-pointed yellow star. Underneath, a blond goddess pours out the elixir of life into a body of water and onto the Earth. She holds a jug of magic potions in each hand. Her right foot dances lightly on top of the water.

MEANING:

The Star represents hope. Wishes come true. Perseverance unites with vision and creates a template for success. The Star's brilliant light guides the way through life's obstacles.

STAR SIBS

Kevin Kline 10-24
Monica 10-24
Joaquin Phoenix 10-28
Dylan McDermott 10-26
Sylvia Plath 10-27
Julia Roberts 10-28
Lauren Holly 10-28
Winona Ryder 10-29
Nia Long 10-30
Dermot Mulroney 10-31
Toni Collette 11-1
David Schwimmer 11-2
k.d. lang 11-2
Roseanne 11-3
Kathy Griffin 11-4
Matthew McConaughey 11-4
Ethan Hawke 11-6
Jeremy and Jason London 11-7
Gretchen Mol 11-8
Parker Posey 11-8

Heather Matarazzo 11-10
Calista Flockhart 11-11
Demi Moore 11-11
Leonardo DeCaprio 11-11
Nadia Comaneci 11-12
Whoopi Goldberg 11-13
Jonny Lee Miller 11-15
Oksana Baiul 11-16
Martha Plimpton 11-16
Daisy Fuentes 11-17
Isaac Hanson 11-17
Elizabeth Perkins 11-18
Chloë Sevigny 11-18
Owen Wilson 11-18
Peta Wilson 11-18
Meg Ryan 11-19
Jodie Foster 11-19
Jason Scott Lee 11-19
Kerri Strung 11-19
Sabrina Lloyd 11-20

COSMIC ADVANTAGES

Original

Psychic

Fervent

Telepathic

Passionate

Compassionate

Intense

Persistent

Understanding

Consistent

Intuitive

Creative

Profound

Sensitive

Visionary

Enthusiastic

Zealous

COSMIC CHALLENGES

Compulsive

Irrational

Cynical

Overly dramatic

Manipulative

Pessimistic

Dejected

Misunderstood

Sad

Uncontrollable

Depressive

Secretive

Unhappy

Negative

Gloomy

Obsessive

Wallowing

SAGITTARIUS
NOVEMBER 22 – DECEMBER 21

RULING PLANET:
jupiter

SYMBOL:
the archer

SEASON:
fall

QUALITY:
mutable

ELEMENT:
fire

COLORS:
royal blue and power purple

POWER STONES:
turquoise, lapis lazuli

BODY:
thighs and hips

FLOWERS:
narcissus, carnation

CITIES:
toledo, washington, d.c., budapest, sheffield, and cologne

VIBRATION:
adventurous, free-spirited, and outdoorsy

COUNTRIES:
spain, australia, and hungary

ZODIAC HOUSE:
ninth

KEY WORDS:
i explore, seek, and search for the truth.

WHAT AM I LIKE?

SAGITTARIUS IS THE COSMIC ADVENTURESS.

Happy-go-lucky. Starstruck. Sagittarius is the Zodiac's most spiritual vibration. Your need for mind-expanding experiences propels you on a **lifelong** quest. It's as if the cosmos whispers in your ear, directing you from one exploit to the next.

Of the three Fire signs, you are the most **evolved.** Optimistic, lucky, and extroverted, you crave movement. Confined spaces, routine places, and uptight faces drive you nuts.

You **intuitively** know how to live life. Never satisfied with pat answers, you believe things can always improve. Your visualizations guide you into the unknown. But you never question your urge to chase after the intangible when your intuition is strong.

You see the Big Picture. People are drawn in by your charisma. Sagittarius is the sign of the Benevolent Dictator. Typically, you wind up in a power position, where your sphere of influence is considerable. You know how to make others want to work for you.

Once you touch somebody's life, you stay with them forever. You have a **dynamic** affect on people. A word, gesture, or **impromptu** pep talk could change someone's life for the better. And you're always shocked to find out you made a difference because you weren't really trying.

This constant movement creates problems for you in the **friend department.** Despite your gift of making friends instantly, no one gets close. It's hard for people to know the real you because you're always on the run.

You don't do this deliberately, either. It's not that you don't want to sit still, it's just that you can't. There always seems to be something you need to do. You can't commit if you always have to **split.**

This elusive quality only makes people want you more, which explains why you have so many friends. You can devote only so much time to each person from the vast network of friends you've collected from all your adventures.

But how many people do you confide in? Intimacy and **opening up** isn't your style. Sure, you're outgoing to the nth degree, but you keep things light.

Human nature fascinates you. You will strike up a conversation with anybody just to see what makes them tick. But when somebody pins you down, you get restless. You feel like you're missing out on something more interesting.

Spontaneous and athletic, you despise confinement. You can't wait to tear off your school clothes the second you walk in the door, leaving a trail of clothes on your way to your room. You're practically claustrophobic.

You don't understand how anyone puts themselves into a rut. You simply cannot relate.

Dizzy with the moment, you plunge in and never look before you leap. You make expensive mistakes by not thinking things through. No matter what the price is, you never regret what you've learned. In your mind, it's the only way to live. It's how you learn, even if it hurts. And you're always **philosophical** about the outcome.

The built-in wanderlust that permeates every single cell in your body explains why so many Sagittarians lead storybook lives.

MY ASTRO HOUSE

YOUR NATURAL HOUSE IS THE NINTH HOUSE. It represents higher education, religion, spirituality, foreign countries, long journeys, and the publishing world. It explains your **inborn** thirst for experience.

The ninth house mindset gives you vision to spot opportunities where other people can't. It always **amazes** you when people can't see destiny staring them in the face.

With challenges of any kind, your attitude is, **"Bring it on,** I can do it." And you do! The harder, the better.

When you don't succeed at something the first time out, you want it even more. This makes you an awesome athlete and a fierce **competitor.** Reality goes out the window when it comes to ambition. To you, the rules don't apply. You know they're there, but your way is bigger, better, and braver.

The last thing you are is a quitter.

Remember how bruised and bloody your knees got the first time you rode a two-wheeler in elementary school? You gave your parents a heart attack, but no matter how many times you fell, you kept on going until you got it right. Even then, they knew they were in for a **wild ride** when it came to you.

Fast-forward to your current state of affairs. You want to see the world. Sure, you love your home, your town, your family, but the way you see it, the clock is **ticking.** You need to see as much as possible in the least amount of time.

You question the way things are. You could stay in school a really long time before you figure out what you want to do. You may even decide you want to stay in an academic environment the rest of your life.

On the other hand, you may choose a **path** very early on that doesn't require schooling, like sports. You'll quit school to start training right away.

If you're a musician or actress, the same thing is true. You will figure out a way to leave school relatively young in order to start your career. You may regret it later but the way you see it, the world is your classroom. Human nature is your teacher. **Experience** is your major.

HOW DOES MY PLANETARY RULER, JUPITER, AFFECT ME?

JUPITER IS AN ENORMOUS PLANET. HUGE!

How does it influence you? Jupiter is the planet of **luck.** You always seem to be in the right place at the right time. The idea of failing barely ever enters your mind.

Jupiter gives you prosperity consciousness. You **trust** the universe will give you what you want, eventually.

You want more because you know there is more. You're a real risk taker. You are daring. You **seize** life by the throat. You do what's necessary to get what you want. And you usually get it.

You go the distance to face your fears. The way you see it, by confronting your demons, you get rid of excess baggage. Having Jupiter as your ruling planet makes you an inner winner.

The only problem Jupiter creates is in the area of **excess** and overindulgence. That thing within that tells you when you've gone too far, eaten too much, or overdone something. You could do something excessively for years before you finally bottom out and do a 180-degree turn and change your behavior.

Jupiter loves the **dating, mating, romance** dance. You're a terrific and very willing player. The challenge of someone new ignites your fire and awakens your Archer spirit. And you thought Cupid had all the arrows!

You are **bold** in love. Your fearless moves shock even your closest friends. You love the thrill of the chase. Nothing, absolutely nothing, scares you off.

Astro Insight

Unlike the more conservative signs, you don't have that internal radar which blazes fire-engine red and tells you when it's time to STOP! Do Not Pass Go!

Sagittarius

MY FAMILY

IN YOUR NATURAL HOROSCOPE, mystical Pisces is on your domestic angle. This mystical vibration enhances your natural **open-mindedness.** You gravitate to the poetic, exotic, unusual, artistic, or things that can't be explained in the ordinary way.

Your home life could be chaotic in a creative way. Everyone kind of does their own thing. You may spend a lot of time unsupervised, which means all your **friends** love coming to your house! There could also be some real space cadets at home, the weirder the better.

You are very **accepting.** Your house can be a truly spiritual place. Even though your parents or stepparents have legit jobs now, they grew up in the sixties, the seventies, or the greedy eighties. They may be ex-hippies or ex-yuppies who haven't really grown up yet. You may not even go through a rebellious period because there is really nothing to rebel against. Your spirituality is enhanced by the **magical place** you call home.

WHAT SHOULD I BE DOING

YOU ARCHERS SEE OPPORTUNITY EVERYWHERE.

You can wrap your mind around any idea and visualize yourself doing that particular thing.

If opportunities are not there to begin with, you **create** them. In the course of your life, you will have many different jobs. Or you'll find a job that allows you to be in constant motion, traveling and meeting people on a daily basis. Like working on films that go to different locations. Or being out in the field for a corporation. Or being on the road.

CAREER

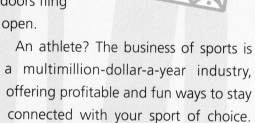

WHY NOT JOT DOWN your deepest desires and make a wish list? Go after internships in the field of your dreams. Internships are resumé builders and put you on the inside. What you think is real **glam** may turn out to be a real snore.

You need to be **on the move.** A tedious office job will drive you nuts in under a week.

The ninth house represents the publishing world. You may get lucky in the high stakes of the book and magazine world. New York awaits! Whether you are an aspiring writer, editor, graphic designer, or a budding style guru, doors fling open.

An athlete? The business of sports is a multimillion-dollar-a-year industry, offering profitable and fun ways to stay connected with your sport of choice. **Promoting** sporting events or working in advertising for a major brand brings you into contact with world-renowned athletes.

Your outgoing personality and entrepreneurial spirit is appreciated in the world of sports, entertainment, and anything that demands **vision** and **fearlessness.**

WITH MY LIFE?

Working in a **fast-paced** environment suits your personality.

There are so many options these days that nothing can prevent you from pursuing your dreams but your own insecurities.

Your **expansive,** can-do spirit cannot wait to take on the world.

Defeat is not a word in your vocabulary. Your hunger for experience leads you in different directions and connects you with many people on your quest for self-realization. Over time, you'll get hip to what makes you happy.

STAR TIPS ON FASHION, HEALTH, AND BEAUTY

YOUR FLYING COLORS? Topaz, tigereye, turquoise, princess purple, lavish lavender, gingerbread, angelic amethyst, Emerald City.

Your **wardrobe** should reflect your free spirit. Your hair should be equally marathon—ready as well as good-to-go for that major date.

Action is your middle name, the outdoors is your home. Saturate yourself with skin-friendly sunblock now to avoid exposure problems later. Sag is **all about travel,** so stock up on travel-sized goodies. Rehydrators transcend time zones, sea water, UV rays, and sleep deprivation.

Develop cosmetic consciousness and implement a "less is more" philosophy. Use noninvasive foundation and easy-does-it lipstick. Only blush when you *see him*.

CUSP KIDZ

SCORPIO-SAGITTARIUS:
NOVEMBER 19-23

Intense Scorpio merges with spirited Sagittarius to create the **Cusp of Passion.**

Scorpio's secretive nature fuels Sag's desire to grasp life's mysteries. You demand **honesty** from others, but never quite reveal your own hand. You always know just how to play out a situation to your advantage.

Scorpio's relentless drive to find answers and get to the bottom of things is tempered by your **supercool** Sagittarius style that skyrockets you to stardom. A dynamic cosmic combo!

SAGITTARIUS-CAPRICORN:
DECEMBER 19-23

Have you ever just known something before it happens? It could be something as inconsequential as thinking about someone seconds before you get the call. Ever wonder where you get this gift of prophetic thinking? This kind of **ESP?**

A Sagittarian's spiritual radar morphs with a Capricorn's uncommon sense of how things work to create the **Cusp Of Prophecy.** You have a sixth **sense.** People and places feel fated. It is as if nobody is in your life by mistake. Dèjá-vu and psychic flashes happen on a regular basis and make you feel like there is a rhyme and a reason to it all.

COSMIC LOVE MATCHES

SAGITTARIUS–SAGITTARIUS
WONDER-LUST

This same sign combination can be even more fun than you, the **starry-eyed** young lady, could hope for. You have much in common, specifically the Zodiac's fortune cookie, lucky **Jupiter.**

You are both eager for things to work and you put **110 percent** into making it happen. You start this love match with high hopes that it will be a billion times better than your last love link. In fact, you Archers almost always forget how bad the last one was because you are entirely focused on the present.

Your intuition about each other is strong.

As Sagittarius you both love sports and the outdoors, and probably won't try to tie the other one down. You need to be **mobile.**

Even if this love link doesn't last, your mutually philosophical outlook enables you to stay friends long after the infatuation **fizzles** out. Hey, you shared an amazing experience, you're going to want to talk about it, right?

Astro Insight

You both need space. He can be dominating, but so can you. You are both convinced that your way is the right way. It can spin you out for days if the other person won't see things your way.

SAGITTARIUS–AQUARIUS
PLANET FUN

You're Fire and he's Air. Boy, does he fan your flame.

Just like most of the male population, he needs his **space,** but you need even more. The Aquarian male is not interested in mind games and is **honest** about what he likes about you.

Most Aquarians are beyond peer pressure and macho garbage. He's a real original. The nice thing about you two is how mature you two can be as a couple.

He's **chilly** Winter, which makes him reserved, single-minded, and fixed in purpose. You are late Fall and very evolved. This is a relationship in which you are both motivated to grow.

But his Fixed quality could cause an itsy-bitsy problem for you. Your **mutable** quality makes you **flexible** and open-minded. Your male of the moment is pretty inflexible about his opinions.

SAGITTARIUS–CAPRICORN
BELOVED OR BEDEVILED?

You can be just what the doctor ordered for your mountain-climbing male Capricorn. Your **unrelenting spirit** is infectious and opens him up in a way he never imagined. Mostly because he never expected it.

In his loner mind-set, he believes he came into this world alone and that is the way he is leaving it. He doesn't think he needs anyone. He's fine by himself, thank you very much.

The **proximity** between your two Sun signs bodes very well for this matchup, because you probably share those oh-so-important personal planets. You both see the **Big Picture.**

Mr. Ambition probably has his future already mapped and it may include you. When you earn his trust, look out! Loyal to the bone, he will do everything in his power to show how much he appreciates you.

Turnoffs? You may feel annoyed when he doesn't respond to your spontaneity. He is used to keeping his own counsel.

Some Caps can be cheap. Pay attention at the beginning to how he handles his money. You **Archers** hate penny-pinching. It goes against your prosperity consciousness.

If he is this way now, it's only going to get worse later. Lose

Astro Advice

Find out if certain things you strongly believe are important to him, too. It may not seem like an issue now, but his convictions are so strong that if you disagree on something later, you may never really feel comfortable with him.

Astro Tip

Take it slow. Patience is your biggest challenge. The male Cap is famous for his ability to wait out a situation until the timing is right. If you take things too fast, he may back off just as quickly. He is the walking definition of caution and likes to know who he is dealing with.

He's ahead of his time, thinking of the future, and unpredictable. You're one of the few signs who can keep up his pace.

He can be very **aloof** and seem disinterested when the truth is, you fascinate him. Your effervescent spirit keeps his interest.

And the beauty of it all is that you are only **being yourself.** He sparks to the spontaneity that oozes from every pore of your fearless soul.

SAGITTARIUS–PISCES
CORNERSTONE OF CREATIVITY

As explained in "My Family," Pisces is **mutable** like you. And mystical where you are spiritual.

This love link can be extremely promising. The only issue you might encounter is that since he has one foot in this world and one foot **God-knows-where,** you may have to make sure he checks into the planets' atmosphere once in a while.

Since he is a Water sign, he can be astonishingly **creative.** His poetry, music, or writing could blow your mind. He may even depict you in a story or a song. Pisces hits your point of self-esteem, and he can make you feel really **safe** just by being close by.

Your signs form a 90-degree aspect called a "square," which means your approach to life is very different. He's a challenge but he also brings out the **best** in you.

A Pisces male is tapped into his feminine side and doesn't care what anybody thinks. He feels that his creativity is a celestial channel. He's not very egocentric, just preoccupied. This side is like a blast of **fresh**

Astro Alert

He feels everything. His sensitivity level can be too much, so he seeks to escape. When he goes to his dark, dark place, no one can reach him. Let him be. When he gets it together, make sure he knows you're his friend. This, he will hear.

SAGITTARIUS–ARIES
SIZZLE AND SCORCH

When you two combustible Fire signs fuse, flames of **infatuation** flare almost daily. This classic astro combo feels right almost immediately, but before you relax, know your ram!

Every astrology book or magazine guarantees that this Fire trine is a sure thing. And it may work out for the long haul. That is, if he can deal with your **noncommittal** style and how fast he sprints through life.

When it works, there's nothing like it in the world. His **charisma** complements your vivacity. You're both athletic and competitive, and enjoy similar things. He can crack you up when he wants to.

His moods are 1) busy and 2) in a rush. Pure energy, he's the first burst of Spring.

SAGITTARIUS–TAURUS
CATCH ME IF YOU CAN!

So, here's this earthy, handsome, and grounded Taurus in your face and he's not budging. It's goose-bump time, girl. No amount of running away and playing hard to get will work on him because he is going to wait very patiently until he gets an answer. He **dares** you to relax your grip on the world.

This is an **unusual** combination. You're elastic, flexible, and ready to jump at the slightest hint of excitement. He's steady, dependable, and every-thing else can just wait until he's finished with what he's doing. He is slow on the uptake but when he makes up his mind, that is that. Period. You change your mind as often as you change channels at a commercial break. He's grounded, but you fly!

You search for **new ways** to do things. You reinvent the wheel. You have this nasty little habit of fleeing the scene when things get too heavy. The male Bull in infatuation mode is quite **adorable** and sweet, so sit back, put your feet up, and take what he so freely gives.

Astro Glitch

His slow-motion style could drag you down and hold you back. Your consistently high spirits could unnerve him over time and drive him away. He's mellow. You're manic. Neither of you will change. Ever.

He's **hotheaded** and reckless. As a Fall sign, you're more reflective. You wonder how things work. You think about **cause** and **effect.** He thinks about how to use what's already there for his advantage. He **dashes** through the urban jungle, paving the way for you both to continue your adventure.

Cosmic Clue

Aries is so very, very me, me, more about me. He's sweet when he needs something. But he never does anything unless it will benefit him. You can really learn how to take care of yourself by watching how he operates.

SAGITTARIUS–GEMINI
MIRROR, MIRROR

Your solar opposite is **adorable,** verbal, and **inquisitive.** It's like looking in a mirror. You are, but there are personality differences you should be aware of.

The main difference? Gemini is **childlike,** a Spring baby who gets into everything and is emotionally shortsighted. Fun? Yes. An old soul? Far from it. You are a philosophical sophisticate. A Fall sign committed to change. You see the Big Picture.

Your mutual flirtation skills and ability to keep things light is a common denominator in the arithmetic of infatuation.

You're both continually in transit. You're on a profound spiritual search, he sightsees in search of the Kodak moment.

He makes life seem like a nonstop party. Together you pull out all the stops. You both love a good time and it's like you have a best friend and boyfriend rolled into one.

You both have short attention spans and a roving eye. **Long-term** commitment is unlikely, but if there's a deep connection, you may remain in touch and be there for each other as you weather the storm of the relationship lottery.

Whether or not this love link lasts, it ranks way up there as the best entertainment you've had so far.

SAGITTARIUS–CANCER
SATELLITE OF LOVE

He's a Cardinal Water sign, meaning he acts on emotions. This wouldn't be so perplexing if you could decode his many moods, but the Moon Child is impossible to figure out.

His ruling planet, the Moon, moves in mysterious ways. So does he. You're an **open book,** almost tactless in your brazen honesty. He's hard to read, as everything he does is cloaked in secrecy.

He keeps things bottled up. He thinks his emotions make him weak. He's imaginative, but controls how he comes across.

SAGITTARIUS–LEO
FIVE-ALARM ATTRACTION

Welcome to your fantasy man. With a Leo in your life, you always do everything to the max. He goes after things with the same enthusiasm as you. He lives for love. **Romance** is his favorite sport.

He loves how passionate and involved you get about the things in your life. You love how uninhibited he is. With the Lion King, it's red carpets, red roses, and you're ready to rock. He loves to show you off.

Face it, you can be a little scatterbrained as you rush around, doing life in your "now you see me, now you don't" fashion. Always **on the run,** there's bound to be a few details that fall through the cracks.

It is part of your charm and what grabbed his royal attention and affection. He knows you're in his league.

Your Fire signs form the celestially rewarding trine.

He's Fixed Fire. His **opinions** are unwritten law. He's fierce about seeing things a set way. He gives everything of himself when it comes to friendships and love. He expects the same loyalty in return. Your noncommittal and elusive manner could frustrate him. He may just be the thing to **slow you down.**

He frequently lapses into vanity or conceit mode. He needs care, feeding, flattery, and stroking. But he's so **dynamic** and **lovable,** it's impossible to stay annoyed.

You make him see how silly he can get without being insulting. You tease each other. The **good news?** You're both straight shooters, so there probably won't be unpleasant surprises as time passes.

Astro Hint

It takes effort to make this love match last since you're so different. You never know when you hurt his feelings and he won't tell you. He'll get sulky and moody and expect you to read his mind.

He envies your spirit and spontaneity. Your open-mindedness amazes him. He cannot imagine being so spontaneous. You literally **rock his world.**

Your influence could make him feel safe enough to crawl out of his crab shell. His influence could make you consider how you're affecting others on an emotional level.

He is self-protective and sensitive. He cannot bear getting hurt. So, be nice.

SAGITTARIUS–VIRGO
WORLD TRAVELERS

Even though your attitudes are remarkably different, you're both Mutable signs, signs that **transform** the energy of one season to the next. This love link is supposed to be doomed, but there are rules of attraction that could make this work.

Virgo analyzes, criticizes, and dissects. An Earth sign, Virgo is consumed with how things work and what makes people tick. Virgos live to work. They are perfectionists. Even though you look for the Big Picture and hate to be bogged down with the very same details that fascinate a Virgo, you're both inquisitive. He can fill in the blanks and make you understand yourself in a more practical way.

How many times have you **rushed** headlong into something because you felt like it and really didn't know why? Your **spontaneity** could remind him that he needs to live a little bit more. You can expand his mind like a rubber band and make him see how big the world is.

In love, he's **careful,** discriminating, and secure. His responses surprise you. Your bold moves scare him at first, but he'll get used to it. You intrigue him. He digs that you are a **work in progress** and he'll never really finish figuring you out.

SAGITTARIUS–LIBRA
BREATH OF FRESH AIR

This Air–Fire coupling is a **superb** blend of energies.

The only thing that could make this a short-term love link? **Libras** are in love with the idea of being in love. You may discover they really don't know you, but are crazy about the person they think you are.

You Archers are a **walking Discovery Channel.** You usually hit the road after the appetizer, rarely waiting for the entrée to be served.

You're Mutable Fire; he's Cardinal Air. Cardinal signs make things happen. He **adores** your attitude and optimism. To an intellectual Air sign your philosophical way of seeing things is a turn-on. Your "now you see me, now you don't" tactic challenges the romantic in him. He makes you think things through. He shows you the **importance** of making a commitment.

SAGITTARIUS–SCORPIO
TOO CLOSE FOR COMFORT

You're both Fall spirits and probably share those **critical personal planets** that are beneficial aspects of a love link. Like Mercury, Venus, and Mars.

When you have the most **passionate** Water sign of the Zodiac in your life, take it seriously. Find out your Rising sign for a more comprehensive picture of your personality traits. With Scorpio, **information is power.**

Scorpio is a born detective. When he likes you, he may start giving you the third degree, because he feels he has to know absolutely everything about you. You are his new project.

This can be flattering at first because he makes you feel like you're the only person on Earth. But be careful, Scorpio can be sneaky and underhanded. Especially if he's consumed with you. Even though you could like him a little, his **intensity** kind of freaks you out.

On the good side, his focus enables you to target what you want from life. The number of possibilities does not seem so overwhelming. If the affection is **mutual,** you can be awesome allies. This relationship goes deep and feels like destiny.

So, enjoy your **Karma King.** You are the spiritual and philosophical goddess who rocks his world. A Scorpio will take you on a trip of a lifetime.

Astro Alert

The odd Libra is more in love with himself than he is with you. If this is the case, hand him a mirror as a parting gift. He'll get the message.

He's good for your **ego.** He'll let you know what he likes about you. He can be very demonstrative when you are alone. He may not be as spontaneous as you but he can keep up the pace. He knows you don't care what other people think, so he feels free enough to show PDA: **public displays of affection.**

MY TAROT CARD
The Ace of Wands

IMAGE:

Depending on the deck, there are several different images that depict the Ace of Wands. In one deck, a disembodied hand emerges from the clouds, holding a leafy single wand way above the Earth. It bears lush, very green leaves.

In another deck, it is drawn with bright colors: oranges and yellows. Flaming, curling flames form a gorgeous, symmetrical pattern.

MEANING:

Wands is the suit of the tarot, symbolizing movement and action. An Ace signifies fresh starts. Creativity. Imagination. Invention. It portends the beginning of all good things. New ideas and the starting point of fresh enterprises.

Drawing this card is evidence of a lifelong lucky streak. You'll always get a second chance to correct mistakes. The universe works for you. Have faith in your abilities. If you make mistakes, chalk them up to experience. Nobody's keeping score but you. Who cares if you scrape your knees trying?

STAR SIBS

Jena Malone 11-21
Boris Becker 11-22
Christina Applegate 11-25
Dougray Scott 11-25
Amy Grant 11-25
Tina Turner 11-26
Jon Stewart 11-28
Gena Lee Nolin 11-29
Kim Delaney 11-29
Ben Stiller 11-30
Tracey Austin 12-2
Britney Spears 12-2
Brendan Fraser 12-3
Tyra Banks 12-4
Marisa Tomei 12-4
Nick Stahl 12-5
Sinead O'Connor 12-8
Kim Basinger 12-8

Jakob Dylan 12-9
Emjay 12-9
Nia Peoples 12-10
Rider Strong 12-11
Mayim Balik 12-12
Jennifer Connelly 12-12
Bridget Hall 12-12
Jamie Foxx 12-13
Wendie Malick 12-13
Benjamin Bratt 12-16
Milla Jovovich 12-17
Katie Holmes 12-18
Ray Liotta 12-18
Casper Van Dien 12-18
Brad Pitt 12-18
Jennifer Beals 12-19
Amy Locane 12-19
Alyssa Milano 12-19

COSMIC ADVANTAGES

Daring

Enthusiastic

Lively

Active

Determined

Fearless

Lucky

Animated

Dynamic

Feisty

Open-minded

Athletic

Eager

Fervent

Philosophical

Bold

Energized

Gutsy

Spirited

Courageous

Vibrant

Vigorous

Vivacious

COSMIC CHALLENGES

Agitated

Defiant

Irritable

Always "on"

Dominating

Rebellious

Last-minute

Ambiguous

Impatient

Noncommittal

Rough

Belligerent

Phony

Scatterbrained

Ingenuous

Spurious

Blunt

Prone to exaggerate

Superficial

Insincere

Restless

Deceptive

Unreliable

Sagittarius

222

SIGNS OF WINTER

CAPRICORN, AQUARIUS, AND PISCES

THE WINTER SPIRIT

IN WINTER, DARKNESS ECLIPSES THE LIGHT.

The night itself has a presence. It's as if we've returned to the **womb.** We stay indoors. We sleep longer. The sun becomes a stranger.

Nature hibernates. It's the dark night of the soul. We **reflect.** We rest. We **dream.** The increasingly cold winds slow everything down. The Earth conserves and restores its energy.

During Winter we take stock of our lives. Holidays remind us of what and who is important to us.

Winter reflects the spirit of celebration. Of ringing out the old and bringing in the **new.** We think about what exists and decide what we need. We plan, envision, and imagine the future.

Winter signs are Visionaries.

Capricorns visualize their place in the scheme of things relatively young. Everything they do in their life is aimed toward fulfilling their vision of what they should be. No matter how difficult the obstacles in their path may be, they eventually prevail.

Aquarians visualize how to **improve** upon existing systems. Driven by their vision and genius, they cannot be swayed from their purpose.

Mystical Pisces visualizes a better world. They give **selflessly** of themselves to make the world a better place. Whether they help the needy with the grace of an angel, or they use their creativity for positive things, they are the link between this world and the next.

You Winter signs are the most evolved of the Zodiac. You possess wisdom and insight beyond your years. You're old souls. You know things that the other seasons can't begin to understand.

You can sustain efforts toward a goal over a long period of time. Once you know what your dream is, you have the strength of mind and will to attain that goal, no matter what.

Let's say it's something like dance. You eventually want to be on Broadway or in a major ballet company. If it's a competitive sport, your goal is the Olympics or playing professionally. If it's writing, you want to be published. Winter signs will **resolve** to do what it takes over a lifetime to study, perfect technique, and face rejection until they get a major break.

You Winter babies have the patience to wait things out. You have that inner conviction to know that your time will come. No amount of setbacks or rejections could change your mind.

You are cautious. You observe. Because your sense of **timing** is so good, you create your own luck. The earlier signs act on their deep need for attention, while you tend to be more reserved.

The universe singles you out to undertake **significant** projects. Your big dreams seem fated. You attract others to help you carry out your vision.

Though your dreams are personal, you know others will **benefit** from your work.

CAPRICORN

DECEMBER 22 – JANUARY 20

QUALITY:
cardinal

RULING PLANET:
saturn

SYMBOL:
the sea goat

SEASON:
winter

COLORS:
ivy, gray, mink, and sage

FLOWERS:
purple carnation, cactus flower, and daffodil

ELEMENT:
earth

COUNTRIES:
india, mexico, iceland, and russia

BODY:
skin, teeth, and knees

POWER STONES:
turquoise, amethyst, and topaz

VIBRATION:
determined, focused, and witty

ZODIAC HOUSE:
tenth

CITIES:
oxford (u.k.), brooklyn, mexico city, washington, d.c., and toronto

KEY WORDS:
i am ambitious and patient enough to achieve my goals.

WHAT AM I LIKE?

YOU ARE A CARDINAL EARTH SIGN WITH INFINITE DRIVE. You may be good at hiding your ambition, but the people who know you sense you'll reach the **heights** of dizzying success.

Part of succeeding is knowing how to lose and deal with set-backs. You are adept and mature when faced with apparent failure. In fact, you learn from them and, as a result, don't even see them as failures. More than any other sign, being a Capricorn means that your life is a series of **karmic lessons,** doled out from your ruling planet Saturn.

Nothing in the life of a Capricorn is random or meaningless. Every person, place, or thing that crosses your path teaches you something. You may not have much fun with many of these lessons but you endure them just the same.

You are extremely patient. You wait your turn. You never doubt

that you'll get what you want, eventually.

Your timing is usually excellent. You have the **discipline** and talent to turn your dreams into reality. In fact, you believe day-dreaming is a waste of time unless you do something about it.

You can be a real loner. Even if you are surrounded by friends, you can feel this way. You

recoil when people offer help. Your independent, self-sufficient attitude always says, Thanks, but I can do it myself. Asking for help is hard for you to do.

Capricorns have the **driest** sense of humor of all the signs. Even though you are usually sober, serious, and solemn, your wit saves the day.

You always provide comic relief when it is needed most. This is also where your sense of timing excels.

You rely on **friendships** more than most signs since you are a loner. They balance you. You like spring and summer signs because they reconnect you to the part of you that craves fun. Fall and Winter signs relate to your depth.

Capricorn can feel more unwanted, left out, and alienated than most signs. You tend to believe the worst, get depressed, and withdraw inside yourself. You can think, What's the point?, and **isolate** yourself.

It takes a truly understanding and persistent person to break the impenetrable walls of your defenses. If they only knew how much you appreciate their attempts to get near you, it would blow their mind.

Astro Tip

As you age through your twenties and beyond, you will be happy to know that the aging process reverses for a Capricorn. You truly get better as you grow older. On the inside as well as the outside.

Capricorn is more aware of the importance of **popularity** and social standing than any other sign. Since Saturn is the guiding force behind the structure of things, you naturally see the world in terms of who goes where. You know what status and recognition can do for you. Therefore, you are very **selective** in choosing your friends. You know you are judged by who you know.

Being impulsive is hard since you're so cautious. You think things to death! You look for wild and spontaneous friends who satisfy your need for excitement.

It's tough for you to **open up.** When you trust someone, they become precious. You can't imagine life without them. They connect you to the world. They may never know how important they are to you.

YOUR NATURAL HOUSE IS THE TENTH. It starts on that "power point" on the very top called the Mid-heaven, ruling your career, so *very* Capricorn.

Your life's ambition is to be **at the top,** no matter what. Rarely does anything fall into your lap, you have to work hard to get what you want.

The traditional definitions attributed to the tenth house are: **public image** or profile, authority figures, the father or any paternal influence in your life, significant mentors, fame, celebrity, publicity, award, scholarships, business, government, career, and achievements with social impact.

During your **teens,** the tenth house translates into such things as gaining popularity, attaining a role of importance in extracurricular activities, and finding an inspirational mentor.

Another thing the tenth house presents is the **father figure.** So what if you are Daddy's Little Girl? Hey, there's absolutely nothing wrong with looking up to him in adoration.

The last thing that your natural tenth house does for you is gives you the stamina to **succeed** in anything that intrigues or interests you. Bumps in the road only serve to redouble your efforts. You are **programmed** for winning. Don't worry if things don't happen right away. Capricorns are late bloomers. Things happen when you're old enough to appreciate them.

HOW DOES MY PLANETARY RULER, SATURN, AFFECT ME?

SATURN IS CALLED
THE COSMIC TIME KEEPER,

because its orbit pinpoints times of change in your life on a predictable timetable.

Saturn takes two and a half years to go through each sign as it moves around the Zodiac. Every **seven** years, Saturn forms an important aspect to its "natal" position (its position in your birth chart).

This transit triggers important events that change your life forever. A new school. A new relationship. A new house. When you're **older,** its influence is even more significant. It could mean a new job in a new city, new living arrangements, or a marriage.

Saturn cycles affect everyone, but because it is your ruling planet, its effect is intense. Saturn is the **"karma"** planet. The great teacher. It's the "moral of the story." Fortunately, sleek Saturn is in your corner.

Saturn thrusts you into situations designed to test your limits. You grow in spite of yourself. Saturn promises that when you learn a lesson, you'll never have to repeat it.

Saturn also promises that if you keep making the same mistakes, it will keep throwing you into similar situations until you finally learn. Saturn doesn't mess around. It **demands** obedience!

MY FAMILY

You home life is probably **noisy, fun, spirited,** and full of over-achievers. Your parents are usually very enthusiastic about their work, their family, and try to make you as excited about the world as they are.

Your brothers and sisters can be incredibly **competitive** with you and you can feel like you are always scrambling for the attention and approval of your parents. This need to be the **best,** do the **best,** and get the **best** could be very stressful. There never seems to be a time when you can just chill, so you probably find things to get you out of the house.

But getting out of the house is a pre-requisite in your family! Your days, nights, and weekends are chock-full of one **activity** after the next. If you're not playing at least two sports, working on the yearbook, being part of a study group for the SATs, and trying out for the school play, you're not doing enough!

You put your family **first.** They have a huge impact in how you see yourself in relation to the world. Even when you grow up and move out of the house, the voices of your over-achieving family will stay in your head for years to come.

WHAT SHOULD I BE DOING

CAPRICORN IS THE SIGN THAT REPRESENTS CAREER, public profile, and running the show. Knowing you Caps, you've probably mapped out your entire professional life already. A surgeon, a senator, an Academy award–winning actress, a Pulitzer prizewinning writer, the CEO of a corporation. The **bigger** the **better.**

Capricorn

CAREER

CAPS ARE DESTINED TO HAVE AN IMPORTANT CAREER. In fact, your career could be the central relationship in your life. Its importance could override the more personal things, like family or relationships. That's how **devoted** you are. Doors open, opportunities arise, and you're always ready to take on any challenge, no matter how hard or impossible it seems.

You are a political creature. You can look at a work environment and figure out who's who in terms of importance in less than ten minutes. You gravitate toward very **powerful** people.

To a Capricorn, power is an aphrodisiac. You need to be around it, to learn from it, and to possess it.

Therefore, it is important for you to either start your own business where you don't have to work underneath anyone, or find the kind of company or business where there is a very **tall** ladder to climb.

Writer, model, actor, financial advisor, art dealer, editor, or lawyer; no matter what you choose, you hate feeling confined. You need to be **where the action is,** where the deals are made. You need a career where you are working with accomplished people who show you how the world works.

You have **exceptional** luck with career interests. You'll experience several important breaks during your life. If the thing you desire hasn't happened yet, be assured it's only because the universe wants you to wait for something better than you could ever imagine.

WITH MY LIFE?

As an Earth sign, Cap is a realist. But remember, your season spirit is visionary. You're realistic about what exists, but prepared to change the rules.

You can **discipline yourself** to complete a project with zero supervision. You follow your passions. And you really do not care if other people think you're crazy. If Plan A doesn't work, you always have a Plan B.

STAR TIPS ON FASHION, HEALTH, AND BEAUTY

YOU WINTER SOLSTICE SWEETHEARTS GROW YOUNGER AS YOU GET OLDER. Saturn also governs the knees. **Bend** and stretch as you ascend that symbolic mountain that you relentlessly climb on your way to the top. Pay special attention to your teeth and skin since these are also ruled by Capricorn.

With **colors,** you feel weird with flashy or loud colors. You won't let colors wear you—you need to wear them! As an Earth sign, you go for understated-but-bold, conservative-yet-sexy. Stallion brown, cactus olive, desert sand, and dark blue are your favorites. Oh, and **black,** of course!

With your wardrobe, don't let some of those great clothes hibernate. If you have it, wear it. You Caps possess the sophistication to carry anything off, no matter how wild your style. Always tap into your **originality.**

With your hair, anything goes. But you tend to go for the more conservative look. Baby-fine or ultrathick, pageboy, layered, or short and spunky. Ponytail it, part it straight in the middle, or stick it under a baseball cap. Just make sure to keep it clean, **shiny,** and healthy.

With skin and makeup, less is so much more. Whether you have zits or flawless skin, don't keep touching! Oh, and clean your phone regularly. That receiver attracts sweat, lipstick, and makeup like a magnet. Capricorn skin improves over time. Invest in products that last more than a weekend. Quality skin products last at least three months.

CUSP KIDZ

SAGITTARIUS-CAPRICORN: DECEMBER 19-23

How much does it **suck** to never have your birthday in school? If you have really cool parents, they'll overcompensate in the present department because they know how gypped you feel.

So, you'll be happy to find out how **special** it is to be born on this cusp, the most magical, mystical one of them all. This is a present that lasts all year, all your life.

Just like your neighbor on the Sagittarius side of this cusp, it's important you understand that the power of the oncoming sign, Capricorn, eclipses the influence of the exiting sign. This is the Cusp of Perception.

Your senses are highly developed. It's not that you're psychic, it's more like you can sense something before it happens. And you have X-ray vision with other people. You listen to what they say, but always see beyond the words. In addition to this unusual gift of yours, Sagittarian energy brightens your aura.

You have the great Cap traits, like consistency, organizational skills, ambition, and social savvy, but you are not as gloomy as most goats. This dual Sag–Jupiter vibe boosts your **optimism** and makes you philosophical about your destiny.

CAPRICORN-AQUARIUS: JANUARY 18-22

This is the **Cusp of Mastery.** The advantage of being born on this cusp is that Aquarius's electric and **unpredictable** energy flow is stabilized by Capricorn's common sense.

Ideas come to you in **flashes.** You're a rushing train that cannot be stopped. Your mind reels with enthusiasm. You try new things all the time.

With your Capricorn practicality, you're able to carry out your innovative and original ideas in a realistic way. Many people born on this cusp are **trendsetters** who make a cultural mark through the arts, media, or communication.

The Aquarian in you makes you unpredictable. It gives you the gift of telepathy. Things penetrate your conscious mind like a bolt of **lightning.**

COSMIC LOVE MATCHES

CAPRICORN–CAPRICORN
CRUSHING COMPROMISE

The biggest hurdle in this combination is which one of you will make the **first move.** The female Capricorn has just as much difficulty opening up and exposing her feelings as the Capricorn male. This could be a real **stand-off** until somebody caves in and blinks. If your guy is **too luscious to lose,** swallow your ego and image issues for a minute, and let him know you're open for business. He'll be relieved that you've made it easy for him to respond. He could be on the **older** side, and even if he isn't, this bond has a real **serious** and mature feel to it from the very start. You Caps feel uneasy unless you're doing something

goal-oriented. This relationship usually goes in a very **specific** direction.

You could get antsy if no clear direction is stated within the first few weeks or months. It's not so much that you're desperate for a commitment, it's that neither of you can relax unless you both know where you stand.

If he's one of the **good Caps,** he will stick with you no matter what. His devotion goes deep and he doesn't mind seeing you with-out your makeup, in fact he prefers it!

Astro Alert
A few Capricorns are incapable of opening up. He acts cold, remote, and could make you feel that you are not even there. Another kind of Capricorn can be selfish, cheap, and an egomaniac on top of it all. There is zero benefit to sticking around once you've seen his true colors.

CAPRICORN–PISCES
GUILTY PLEASURES

This compatibility mix rates high on the success meter. Pisces–Capricorn is a popular coupling. You're both **winter babies** who are very evolved. He's drawn to your "I've got it all togeth-er" exterior. Your earthy influence gives **form** and **structure** to his watery, wistful ways.

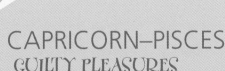

CAPRICORN–AQUARIUS
ELECTRICAL IMPULSE

He blows into your world and turns it **upside down.** He shakes your Capricorn conformity at its very core. He'll force you to break the rules. To take a chance. He surprises you by calling in the middle of the night, making you **swoon** at how romantic life can be. He'll make up secret names for you that only he can use.

Your **Sun signs** are so close, you could have cupid Venus in Aquarius and be able to keep up the pace and even outdo him sometimes. He could have his Venus in Capricorn, which could make you his **ideal** girlfriend. Regardless, you're both Winter signs, and want similar things out of life. You **"get"** each other.

Enjoy him while he's around because the

Aquarians are famous for their **"now you see me, now you don't"** disappearing act. When they have to go, they go. Do not take it personally.

That's why it's so hard for them to form intimate attachments. They know they'll be leaving. It's only a matter of time.

Be **forewarned.** Life with an Aquarius means you should prepare yourself for the emotional hurdle of a long-distance relationship or someone who pops in and out of your life on a whim. And you think you're a loner?

Astro Challenge

As tough as you are on yourself, try to be gentle with your Fish. He is confused most of the time, sensitive, and extremely creative. He's not driven to be a perfectionist like yourself. You can really learn to ease up on yourself and the world around you from him.

His otherworldly appeal pulls you out of your gloomy Capricorn mind-set. His perceptions are so off the wall, you forget to be so serious and find yourself **laughing** again. He makes you happy. It's that simple.

The awesome thing about this combo is that you don't really have to do anything to make it work. That's the **weird logic** of bonding with the magical, mystical fish.

He makes you see how much **fun** you're missing out on. Time with him is a series of

Astro Advice

Enjoy the moment!

stolen moments filled with guilty pleasures. He takes you on a vacation from yourself, your responsibilities, and turns you on to a new way of thinking.

Pisces rules the subconscious, so don't be shocked if he starts appearing in your dreams!

CAPRICORN–ARIES
AN OLYMPIC CHALLENGE

Most astro experts will warn you that this love link is more **trouble** than it's worth, but how could you turn down the awesome Aries? You Capricorns are nothing if not determined to **conquer** and control, and the Ram gives you a run for your money.

He is so hot that you normally composed Capricorns are taken by surprise. Let's get real—the chemistry between you is so powerful, you could cut it with a knife.

He's as irresistible as his season, spring. In a way, that's why you are drawn to each other. He symbolizes the beginning of life. That first atom of energy responsible for creating the universe. And you symbolize the end of the cycle. The first day of Winter when the Earth retreats to conserve itself. You are attracted to his **light.** He is infatuated with your **depth.** It is so foreign to him.

You are both active Cardinal signs and are fated to achieve **great things.** His sunny, impetuous, devil-may-care approach invigorates you. Your conservative, sensible, and mature attitude bewitches him.

No matter how long it lasts, the Ram makes a major impression on your heart. You're so sentimental (not that anyone knows!) that if things end, you could carry a **torch** for a very long time.

Astro Alert

An Aries is a blast at the beginning, but can lose his passion just as fast. And the signs are so there. His eyes roam when you're out. The calls stop. The excuses start. Aries are built for sprints, not marathons. You goats know how to pace yourselves. You always have a good kick in reserve when it comes to finishing the race.

CAPRICORN–TAURUS
COSMIC PLAYGROUND

This coupling is the first of two possible **Earth-to-Earth** trines. This relationship usually develops into a very pleasant experience. When you're around the Spring sign, he makes you feel **cozy** and **safe.** He's more grounded than yourself. He is the real deal.

Rarely do you feel like you're the playful part of the puzzle, but his fixed quality clinches this. He is **stubborn, unyielding,** and set in his ways. Changing his mind is like trying to move a mountain.

You are a Cardinal sign who never lets any

CAPRICORN–GEMINI
REFRESHING AND BUBBLY

This is another cosmic combination that most traditional astrologers will tell you is trouble from the get-go. News flash!

Gemini-Capricorn couples are a favorite when it comes to long-term commitment and marriage. Bubbly **Gemini vibes** revive the somber goat.

Your sensible, sane, and straight-shooting style attracts the Twin. He can learn a lot from you. He **studies** you, trying to absorb your wisdom. Don't be surprised if you catch him quoting you!

The Twin makes you forget your problems. In his presence, you come to life. He **captivates** you.

An evolved Gemini is determined to apply his amazing **intellect** to meaningful things. His idealism and conviction will turn you into a jellyfish. Such noble goals. You're hooked!

grass grow under your feet. You're part of the supernatural Winter season where anything can happen and probably does.

He can be **possessive** and jealous and act like he owns you. This can be flattering at first, but after a while, it could freak you out.

He'll **ease up** if you reassure him about your feelings for him. He can be a brute in an effort to mask his insecurities.

He's great with money. Money is his second language. Giving you gifts and tokens of his affection are the only ways he can talk about the relationship. It's easier for him to give stuff than to say stuff. On the other hand, he could be a real tightwad. Usually, he's pretty balanced.

The bottom line with this combo is that there's very little room or interest for game-playing. You're both **reality-based** Earth signs. You don't fool around when it comes to romance.

CAPRICORN–CANCER
CONTACT SPORT

Your solar opposite is as **cryptic** and complicated as you. Even though you're at opposite ends of the spectrum in many ways, there is an unspoken understanding between you that defies explanation. You are drawn like **magnets** to each other.

Because of this combination's basic complexity, you could be allied for years—the fascination just won't die.

Deciphering his feelings could feel like a **fishing** expedition. With Water signs, body language will tell you far more than words can. When he covers his mouth with his hands, this tells you he's hiding something.

Cancer rules the stomach, so he'll hold his stomach when he's holding back, lying, or just plain uncomfortable.

A Capricorn–Cancer union could make a spectacular bond. Earth and Water mix well and you're both Cardinal signs. You will be productive, goal-oriented, and prone to **powerful emotions.**

When he finally lets his guard down, go with his flow. Obviously, he's emerging from his symbolic crab shell and reaching out. He'll soon show you his **sensitive** and romantic side. Prepare to fall hard!

CAPRICORN–LEO
CELESTIAL GOLD

This crush combination has so many **incredible assets;** you have to pinch yourself to make sure you're not dreaming. Here again we have a combo that most sky watchers will say is a no-no, but there you both are, **starry-eyed** and love-struck. This feisty Fixed Fire sign dazzles you. He's born at the height of the **summer heat** and overpowers your conservative yet capricious Winter ways.

His personality **redefines** the perimeters of your world. You're cautious and **careful.** You never believe good things last.

CAPRICORN–VIRGO
FOR KEEPS

This is the last of the harmonious Earth trines you Caps will encounter on your trek around the Zodiac's romance **merry-go-round.** Your Virgo guy is Mutable Earth. He's picky, intelligent, and **analyzes** everything, including you. You could feel scrutinized, but you kind of like the attention. Even if those sparks don't fly from the start, just wait awhile.

You're secretly waiting for your luck to end.

Even when things are good, you can become **unglued** just thinking about what can go wrong. He makes you believe that life doesn't have to be **predictable** and safe.

He is an **elitist.** The fact that he chose you can't help but make you feel special. When you two are together, you feel like you live in your own world. That everything you say, do, and feel is important and inspired. This could be the start of a **sweeping romance.** You confide everything in each other. You share secrets.

As a surprising **bonus,** he can be a major asset in the fashion and self-esteem department. His style sense is superior. He'll make you change if he thinks you could look better. He'll go through your closet and pick out the exact thing that makes you look **gorgeous.**

And there he is, a best friend and boyfriend rolled into one. Your personal wardrobe consultant! He also excels at advising you how to deal with your **friends.** He can always distinguish what is important from the trivial.

Astro Insight

You're both programmed for success. You like to stay low-profile and behind the scenes. He loves the limelight and wants recognition. You "get" each other and aren't competitive. In fact, you wind up as powerful allies. Miraculously, he doesn't come off conceited because he's so lovable. His loyalty and generosity are famous. Get ready to be spoiled!

CAPRICORN–LIBRA
AMAZING GRACE

This is the last Cardinal crush combo. And it **rules!**
To Libra, love isn't just a **sometime thing,** it's a
way of life. When this perpetual Romeo singles you out for romance,
prepare to fall off your mountain and into his arms.

Say farewell to your orderly way of life. Tap into your capricious Capricorn
side. His Libra allure **enchants** you. You lose track of time. He fills your every
thought. You're walking on air. Mushy lyrics start to make sense. No one bothers
you anymore. Suddenly the world is a **beautiful** place. It's true: he's turned
your world upside down.

Obviously, this **bliss** cannot last forever. Soon, reason and logic return and you
come back down to Earth. This doesn't mean your Libra will disappear. But you
may need to make **adjustments** so you can fit real life in between dates.
Two common denominators exist between your signs. As initiators of a season,
it's like you both run corporations that do business. Your bond is
inescapable.

Secondly, Libras crave frequent periods of solitude in order to
recharge their social battery. They relate to your
"loner" mystique.

CAPRICORN–SCORPIO
FASHIONABLE PASSION

If you're seriously crushing, go to the fall section and devour every word on Scorpio. With the
Duke of Danger, you'll need all the scoop you can get. Decide if you're dealing
with the Scorpion, eagle, or dove and treat him accordingly.

Most Scorpios get a **bad rap,** but you can't see what the big deal is. He sure is sexy,
passionate, and caring. Besides, a Capricorn girl has yet to meet anyone she can't handle.

If you're ambivalent, and he's **interested,** he won't give up without a fight. In fact, the
challenge makes him more determined to win you over. And you can't help but admire

CAPRICORN–SAGITTARIUS
PUSH AND PULL

This combination is a built-in **brain twister.** Your ruling planets, Jupiter and Saturn, represent opposing forces.

Jupiter stands for expansion, **increase,** and **limitless** opportunity. Saturn represents the process of limitations, contraction, and working within an existing structure.

Strange as it seems, you're drawn to each other. Sag needs to learn restraint. You need to relinquish control.

He reminds you that the Universe has something better in store than you could imagine. You provide Sag the structure he needs to truly **succeed.**

He's all about excess. You're all about **necessity.** You keep each other in check.

When he starts to go overboard, projecting big things for your amazing, fantastic, blockbuster of a future, you keep him **on track.** You're optimistic but cautious. You resist getting carried away.

When you get depressed, he reminds you not to take yourself so seriously.

Astro Alert

He can be a real heartbreaker. Once he sinks his arrow of desire in your heart, you're toast. He's a professional flirt. It's not that he lies, but he exaggerates . . . a lot! What you think is a serious conversation about the future can be him simply letting off steam in his famous stream-of-consciousness ramblings.

his attempts. You'll give it a try and say to yourself, "How bad could it be?"

He can make you feel like you're the only girl in the world and treat you like a goddess. But never let down your guard, because he's always planning his next move. He's a **manipulator.** Not always in a bad way, but he's always in the middle of some complicated scheme.

He likes to pounce in the love department. Don't lead him on. He bites back!

MY TAROT CARD
The Wheel of Fortune

IMAGE:

Loaded with symbols, this card draws on the ancient wisdom of Kabbalah (Jewish mysticism), and on Egyptian and Greek mythology as mysterious as the Sphinx.

MEANING:

Knock, knock. Destiny's calling. No silly game show, this Wheel of Fortune is serious stuff.

Ask for the sun, moon, and stars. You will get it. If you hit a dead-end, the cosmos urges you to make a U-turn. With your feet on the ground and your head in the clouds, miracles occur. Just not when you expect them.

STAR SIBS

Ralph Feinnes 12-22
Eddie Vedder 12-23
Ricky Martin 12-24
Jared Leto 12-26
Denzel Washington 12-28
Jude Law 12-29
Tracey Ullman 12-30
Tiger Woods 12-30
Val Kilmer 12-31
Cuba Gooding Jr. 1-2
Christy Turlington 1-2
Mel Gibson 1-3
J. R. R. Tolkein 1-3
Danica McKellar 1-3
Michael Stipe 1-4
Suzy Amis 1-5
Joey Lauren Adams 1-6
Gabrielle Reece 1-6
Katie Couric 1-7

Elvis Presley 1-8
Jenny Lewis 1-8
David Bowie 1-8
Dave Matthews 1-9
A. J. McLean 1-9
Melanie Jayne Chisholm 1-12
Howard Stern 1-12
Julia Louis-Dreyfus 1-13
LL Cool J 1-14
Emily Watson 1-14
Faye Dunaway 1-14
Kate Moss 1-16
Jim Carrey 1-17
Kevin Costner 1-18
Jane Horrocks 1-18
A.A. Milne 1-18
Janis Joplin 1-19
Stacey Dash 1-20
Skeet Ulrich 1-20

COSMIC ADVANTAGES

Determined

Loyal

Ambitious

Firm

Focused

Motivated

Driven

Indomitable

Popular

Skillful

Chic

Initiator

Spirited

Droll

Recognized

Clever

Invincible

Imaginative

Resolute

Stylish

Creative

Traditional

COSMIC CHALLENGES

Witty

Disapproving

Distrustful

Acerbic

Anxious

Disdainful

Guarded

Pessimist

Capricious

Jaded

Reclusive

Skeptical

Condescending

Leery

Sarcastic

Suspicious

Cynical

Loner

Sardonic

Wary

Derisive

Outsider

Shut-down

Worrywart

Devious

Capricorn

2 4 4

AQUARIUS

JANUARY 21 – FEBRUARY 19

QUALITY: fixed

RULING PLANET: uranus

SYMBOL: the water-bearer

SEASON: winter

COLORS: butterscotch, cerulean blue, and ecru

FLOWERS: ambrosia, gladiola, freesia, and snapdragon

ELEMENT: air

COUNTRIES: sweden, belgium, luxembourg, and argentina

BODY: circulatory system and ankles

POWER STONES: aquamarine, opal, and topaz

VIBRATION: innovative and unpredictable

CITIES: akron, st. petersburg, hamburg, montreal, dallas, and pensacola

ZODIAC HOUSE: eleventh

KEY WORDS: i am truthful and an original thinker.

WHAT AM I LIKE?

YOU ARE AN ORIGINAL WITH A CAPITAL "O."

A rebel, a true visionary. Whether you're immersed in the arts or haven't figured out what you want to do when you **grow up,** you never follow the crowd. You don't break the rules in a destructive manner, you just don't think they make much sense. You do your **own thing.**

You are a **true individual** who has her eye on the future. An innovator, you spend your entire life working toward making your vision of yourself and your life real.

You never feel too stuck in any situation because deep down you know that every experience is just a **side street** on the highway of your life.

Aquarius rules the concept of **friendship,** and you spend a tremendous amount of time and energy developing friendships everywhere you go. You pride yourself on being able to **talk** to anyone, whether they're a senior citizen, an exchange student, a professor, a parent, somebody new at school, or

even that little kid next door.

Your friends are **riveted** by your unpredictable nature. They can count on you to come up with the most **outrageous** ideas, shocking opinions, and the wildest schemes. Your sense of humor consistently catches people **off guard.**

You thrive on learning about the world around you, and who better to **teach** you than people who can talk about their backgrounds and experiences?

You like to have a large **network** of friends. You seek high-energy personalities. You're drawn to the Fire and Air signs: they keep up the pace and **stimulate** you. Water and Earth signs tend to be too high-maintenance and heavy, but they fascinate you just the same. You may only be able to take them in **small doses.**

In fact, you hate to

admit it, but as much as you love people, you prefer to be **independent** and on your own. You love humanity in the abstract, but you loathe being part of the **"herd."** It would take a very unusual person to capture your interest over a long period of time.

You're the most unpredictable sign of the Zodiac. Sometimes, *you* don't even know what you're going to do. This trait adds to your allure with the opposite sex. Guys **adore** how unavailable you seem to be. They can never read you. They can't figure out if you're just being polite or you're actually interested. And you're not really sure yourself.

You need to think things out. You don't actually think in the regular way. You're on a different wavelength. You fixate on a subject, ask for clarity, and *boom!* The answers come through. Works every time!

We've been in the "Age of Aquarius" for many years. Aquarius rules electricity, television, technology, radio waves, computers, and telepathy, to name a few.

Has anyone ever seen electricity? It's an invisible energy that makes the world go round. We can't touch it, yet we're completely dependent on it for

Astro Tip

Avoid stress (if possible!). You are far more sensitive than most people, and prone to headaches.

survival and all forms of communication.

As an Aquarius, you have this same energy flowing through your bloodstream, which explains your unusual energy level. All-night cramming doesn't seem to affect you in the same way as other people. When you are **obsessed** with an idea, you may not even feel connected to your body. Your willpower is supernatural.

Aquarius rules the circulation and the nervous system, which includes all the electrical functions of your brain. It is critical that you maintain a healthy brain chemistry by eating properly.

Try what's known as "brain food," like sushi, certain herbs, and lots of protein. In fact, the study of herbs could become a passion of yours.

A born visionary, you are prepared to set the world on fire!

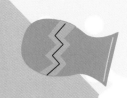

THE ELEVENTH HOUSE IS
CALLED THE HOUSE OF HOPE.

It also represents group efforts, social connections, clubs, unions, associations, unions, teamwork, wishes, aspirations, and dreams.

This explains why you Aquarians usually get involved with school or **community** efforts.

The eleventh house concept is the **expression** of one idea through the combined efforts of a large group of people.

Look at how a movie is made. How many people work on one movie? Hundreds of people join together in the spirit of **collaboration** to carry out one vision. To tell one story.

The **"wish"** factor is omnipresent in the theme of your life. You are convinced that things can always be better. No matter what grim facts or reality stares you in the face, you are committed to a **better world.** Nothing is strong enough to shake your beliefs. When you are committed to a cause, it's for life. Until you find another one to replace it!

In the course of your life, you will probably be presented with many opportunities to join clubs or groups. Your laser-sharp insights **impress** people and you'll probably be asked to lead and be the voice of the group on many occasions.

You always rise to the occasion, because you are **level-headed** enough to know that as much as it is an honor, your job is to suppress your own ego and interests for the good of the group.

HOW DOES MY PLANETARY RULER, URANUS, AFFECT ME?

URANUS IS THE PLANETARY WILD CHILD. It creates chaos, madness, genius, catastrophe, electricity, shocks to the system, and everything **unpredictable.** Uranus never behaves in a conventional way.

As much as it causes disruption, separation, and sudden twists of fate, it also creates flashes of **brilliance,** love at first sight, and strokes of genius.

Uranus takes approximately **seven** years to transit each sign, and over eighty-four years to orbit the Zodiac.

Uranus governs the science of astrology, the television business, radio waves, brain waves, the nervous system, lightning bolts, telepathic thinking, alternative behavior, and the computer age.

Uranus has a strong affect on your personality. You're **avant-garde,** innovative, highly opinionated, and a trendsetter. Your learn superfast. You have above-average intelligence. You're a high-voltage person with a five-hundred-watt smile.

Uranus produces a love for the **unconventional** in your romantic and artistic tastes. The **weirder the better.** You could believe in the supernatural. In alternative healing. In any unusual path toward self-realization.

You love the **New Age.** Anything "middle of the road" puts you to sleep. You crave stimulation and adrenaline rushes. Risky is better. You live on the edge. It's what makes you feel alive. You prefer the thrill of the unknown rather than living a so-called normal life.

You are a person of **extremes.** If you don't think the previous description applies to you, you are probably at the other end of the spectrum and a complete skeptic who refuses to change or open her mind.

MY FAMILY

ACCORDING TO YOUR NATURAL HOROSCOPE, the Fixed Earth sign of Taurus is the anchor to your **domestic** scene.

The normality and predictability of your home life is a major factor in your rebelliousness. It's okay for your parents to stick to a **routine,** play by the rules, and leave no room for surprises, but not for you!

As much as you like to stand out, you **secretly rely** on your family to be there and to be the same, always. It gives you great comfort, although you'd never admit that to anybody.

The truth is, if your home was explosive and unmanageable, you'd probably go the other way and try to hold it all together and be the responsible one.

Taurus is the **money** sign, so it's possible that your family is entrenched in the financial world or that your home is **luxurious.** You could be a very pampered girl and want for nothing.

Your parents could, conversely, always be at you for watching what you spend, paying for your stuff with your own after-school **job,** or lecturing you every time you ask for cash. Either way, in your house, money is an issue.

WHAT SHOULD I BE DOING

AS IF ANYONE COULD TELL YOU WHAT TO DO! Ms. Individualist. Ms. Rebel.

You're an idea-and-concept person. You also gravitate toward those eleventh house affairs requiring **collaboration** and teamwork. And you are intoxicated by the pursuit of freedom and experience.

Aquarius

CAREER

THESE TIMES WERE TAILOR-MADE FOR YOUR PERSONALITY. It's an Aquarian-friendly world. You drive in the fast lane of the information superhighway.

Create you own **dot-com biz** and become a CEO before you turn twenty-five. Plunge into abstract art and indulge your **creativity** creating controversial canvases. Write programs for a Web site or ride the crest of the **Information Age** and be a roving cub reporter. You could find yourself drawn to another eleventh house occupation: working with associations or foundations that raise **money** for important causes. You know how to network. You love to put together **events.** You adore rubbing elbows with the powerful and the **elite.**

Helping others through charitable work fulfills your **humanitarian** needs and can put you in touch with important people who devote their lives to a major cause.

WITH MY LIFE?

Aquarius is the sign of the **altruist.** You know, the lover of mankind, of the people, and for **sweeping causes** that can change the world.

You'll find yourself on a kibbutz, in the Peace Corps, traveling the world to write your **memoirs** before you turn eighteen, volunteering for a presidential campaign, or writing an off-Broadway play.

What should you be doing with your life? You already figured it out. Your only problem is deciding which of **ten brilliant ideas** you should attempt first.

STAR TIPS ON FASHION, HEALTH, AND BEAUTY

IT'S HARD FOR YOU TO STAY BETWEEN THE LINES, and your wardrobe, look, and style reflect your unconventional tastes. You dance to the beat of your own **bongos,** so some peers may think you are a tad weird. And that is just the way you like it. You invent. You experiment. You're independent and ingenious. With colors, vibrant, high-voltage are best. Pastels, all shades of purple from lilac to plums to blueberry. Aquamarine and azure hit the spot.

You strive for **shock value** and could even dye your hair a different color every month, much to the horror of your parents. You could also be tempted to get a little butterfly tattoo on your ankle or pierce your ears all the way up the lobe. You have to make a statement.

You have an interesting relationship with your hair. Sometimes it's just such a drag to maintain it the way it should be, so you keep a ponytail going for over a week. Once you find something you like, it stays. You have zero problem doing drastic things like getting a buzz cut, doing major dreads, or changing color overnight.

With skin care and makeup, find out your skin type—oily, dry, sun-sensitive, blemish-prone—and get into the solution! Natural herbs, plant-extract cleansing milks, and toners help save your skin. Makeup should be **quick, easy,** and emphasize your natural-born beauty.

Since Aquarius governs the bloodstream and circulation, massage those legs with a state-of-the-art body lotion. Make sure you move, on the track, up the stairs, on the court, or in the field.

CUSP KIDZ

CAPRICORN–AQUARIUS: JANUARY 18–22

Capricorn's sophistication merges with Aquarius ingenuity to create the **Cusp of Style.**

You Winter signs are complex creatures, **profound** and **destined** for greatness. Together, these vibrations combine to produce extraordinary individuals committed to their voice, art, and lifestyle.

You possess wit, ambition, clarity of purpose, and mystique. But your path could be a **lonely** one. So few people really get the depth of your faith, belief, and devotion to your work.

The Capricorn in you is very **ambitious** and will never give up. The Aquarius in you won't take no for an answer and has the power to seduce the world with your message and creative gifts.

AQUARIUS–PISCES: FEBRUARY 18–22

As you already know, you Aquarians are telepathic, humane, and have a high IQ. Mix it with **psychic, sensitive** Pisces and you get the **Cusp of the Magi.**

People on this cusp are very successful. Your charm is so beguiling and your **people skills** so refined, that you always get your way. You could be in the public eye. People identify with your struggles and your triumphs. Many popular actors are born on this cusp.

You have **verve, nerve,** and belief in yourself. You come across as so sweet and vulnerable that people fall all over themselves to want to help you. And you know how to work it! You replace that freeze-dried Aquarius **"I don't need you"** attitude by acting out that defenseless Pisces "damsel in distress" role. It works every time.

COSMIC LOVE MATCHES

AQUARIUS–AQUARIUS
THE 411 OF LOVE

No two Aquarians are ever alike, you make sure of that. Your individuality is almost a religion. You **pride yourself** on your ability to befriend the world. You see yourself as a self-proclaimed **anthropologist** or sociologist. You get close enough to ask intimate questions, but you never reveal your own hand.

Put two of you together in a room and let the **games** begin! The success of this love match depends on how willing each of you are to let go, open up, and let somebody in.

The male Aquarius is harder to read, icier, and far more aloof. Where other might love the challenge of trying to **"get him,"** you react much differently. His attitude could turn you off. It's too close to home.

But if you can both get past your **walls of detachment,** you just may find a **stellar playmate.**

You both embrace life and enjoy incredible mental rapport.

More likely? This matchup could resonate with a **brother–sister** vibration. He could be the guy who you call at 3 A.M. to recount your latest dating disaster. He's your best "guy friend," and it only gets better.

The great thing about your mutual detachment is that you avoid wallowing in a murky swamp of emotions. You bounce back fast, ready to **tackle** your next adventure.

AQUARIUS–PISCES
SNOW-BLIND

This is a very **unpredictable** coupling. Because of your proximity and the odds of sharing personal planets, there may not be much of a gap in your characters. **Compatibility** and durability are volatile issues.

AQUARIUS–ARIES
PEDIGREE PERFORMANCE

He could be the **love of your life.** At least for now. You find everything about him attractive, and the rest you simply overlook.

You're both **fast,** confident, **focused,** and refuse to buckle under. In fact, this matchup may be star-crossed in the sense that there is some external force trying to keep you apart. Whether it's the challenge of distance, family disapproval, or as simple as conflicting schedules, you will both strive to make it happen no matter what.

He really gets your **attention.** His impetuous spirit and sheer athleticism have you hooked. You could watch his practices after school, conjuring up creative ways to connect. He's **a guy's guy.** You eat that stuff up. But don't give away too much too quickly.

This is true with most guys, but especially true with an Aries. Remember this and stay tough, or else you'll blow it and beat yourself up. The Ram likes to **stay in control.**

His bad side? He can be **crass,** brash, and extremely **intolerant.** He has zero patience and is emotionally nearsighted. But he's harmless. Sure, he makes a lot of noise, but you can't take him seriously. In this mix, you are the **voice of reason,** and don't think he doesn't notice. He relies on it!

You may not pick up on his moods, his "signals," or know what he needs emotionally. And, he **won't tell** you.

He can't figure you out, either. You're so cerebral that sometimes you walk around feeling nothing at all, just thinking. To him, this is incomprehensible.

But you both can benefit from **bonding.** He reminds you that you live in a world ruled by the heart. This infatuation reawakens the starry-eyed schoolgirl stirrings. You can help him untangle his world and put things in perspective.

Astro Alert

The artistic, emotional, and confused Fish seeks oblivion. If his hobbies are drugs and alcohol, lose him. There are other "fish" in the sea.

AQUARIUS–TAURUS
STUCK ON EACH OTHER

You **deal in ideas,** he deals with what he can touch. You believe in the impossible. He believes in the possible. You're a rebel, he's a realist. How can you two ever **mesh?**

Your Sun signs form an aspect that promotes **instant attraction.** You're drawn together by virtue of these very differences. Very diverse creatures, your first date could be like a day at the petting zoo. You feel each other out. He makes you think. You make him wonder.

So, what could go wrong after the first flush of crush? The Bull is **stuck** in his ways, lazy, and slow. His motto? He'll do it later; it can wait.

You **recoil** from this. Your keen Aquarian mind sees this behavior and detaches immediately. You're allergic to routine.

Ultimately, your Aquarian **eccentricities** can be too much. The Bull likes dependability, a "sure thing," and stability. The only thing he can depend on is the certainty you'll do the unexpected.

His "stuck in the mud" personality could make you **nuts** once the physical attraction loses its grip. Sure, you'll keep him as a friend, but you need somebody who can keep up the **pace.**

AQUARIUS–GEMINI
GET READY FOR TAKEOFF

This Air trine can bring you hours of entertainment, conversation, and a sense that you've met your match. He's an **expert flirt** and brings out the same traits in you. Once you two get going, it's like watching a **screwball comedy.** This is a lighthearted rhapsody and is what infatuations are all about.

Even though you're well aware that, at times, he can be full of it, you enjoy watching him at work. The **chameleon** prince prances and dances right into your heart.

He can be more elusive and unattainable than even you. This is absolutely the kind of relationship you cannot **control,** manipulate, or plan your life around. Since you're

AQUARIUS–CANCER
AN UNSOLVED MYSTERY

Astrologically this is an unlikely coupling, but it happens. He's the epitome of **self-centered** agendas, motives, and emotions. You're the essence of selfless actions and honesty. You devote your life to meaningful causes. So why are you two together and what will happen?

Your Moon child exposes you to **emotional territory** that you didn't even know existed. Somehow, he brings out the part of you that you always push down. Suddenly, you connect to your needs on a more **personal** level. You may immerse yourself in this relationship and commit to self-discovery. He can help you in this respect. He instigated it!

He can bring romance into your life. You're not used to intimacy. You don't know how long you can stand it.

Uranus shocks everything it touches. Since the Moon rules emotions, you could have an unusual influence on him. He may stray from his usual patterns and react spontaneously around you. He could find himself doing things he never thought he could do.

In the long term, you may be too outrageous and upsetting for his sensitive system. And he may be way too heavy and high-maintenance for you to handle.

both flighty, it's anyone's guess how long this will last.

It's not that this is a frivolous thing, it's just that you both always manage to keep things **light.**

Plus, who could let a Gemini get away? They're way too much fun.

Astro Insight
Even if this relationship dies fast, you both are very social and diplomatic people. You'll probably keep the door open for years to come.

AQUARIUS–LEO
BALANCING ACT

This is truly a balancing act between powerful solar **opposites.** Can he keep your interest with his show-off antics? His screams for attention?

Can he relate to your detached **"I don't need anybody"** attitude?

Well, he's up to the job when it comes to you. His ferocious fire melts your **icy airs.** You can't help but fall in love with him. He's too **adorable.** He is the main focus of your extracurricular activities. The Lion is the King of his domain and he chooses you to be his **Queen.**

He loves to be appreciated for his generosity, loyalty, and reliability—all of which he possesses in full. He likes showing you off and going to the hottest clubs. He has this way of making you feel like the **main attraction.**

His downside? He can be proud, egotistical, and demanding. And boy, can he hold a **grudge.** You do not want to be within a mile when he gets mad.

But, there is no reason to be scared. Remember the Lion from *The Wizard of Oz*? A real **pushover** who could barely growl.

AQUARIUS–VIRGO
AMAZING GRACE

Despite the **glaring clash** of a Mutable Earth sign trying to get along with a Fixed Air sign, this combination has an **inexplicable** success rate. It's as if you two are kindred souls.

The reason this works so well is because of the unique mental connection between your two vibrations. Uranus is the **higher octave** of Mercury. You understand each other without explanation.

Even if this Virgo won't be your Mr. Forever, he can be your **Mr. Right Now.**

He's as sharp-witted, shrewd, and verbal as you are. This is the kind of crush that keeps on delivering surprises. You can **talk for hours** on

AQUARIUS–LIBRA
TRINE SUBLIME

This is pure **paradise.** Truly a trine sublime. Together you can experience the definition of new love in all its glory. Take notes so you can remember this once-in-a-lifetime experience.

Libra brings out the **best** in you. He doesn't make you feel misunderstood, misread, or disinterested.

You'd rather have a root canal than expose your feelings. Most people get on your nerves in a very short time. You'd rather reflect on the **"idea"** of someone than find out what they're about in real life.

Libras have a way of getting **under your skin.** They restore your belief in romance. Since they're Cardinal signs, they have no problem initiating contact. Their **irresistible** charm comforts, intrigues, and makes it impossible *not* to respond to their overtures.

They never get **too close.** They give you space without suffocating you. You can become so engaged that it could be you who worries about losing them!

any subject. You understand what you're each trying to **accomplish** in this world, and even though these goals probably differ to an enormous degree, you offer **unconditional support** to each other.

The **downside?** You're both analytical and lead with your head. A cold wind of **detachment,** distance, and modesty could come between you. You're able to maintain animated conversations, but you could both falter and **choke** when it comes to taking it to the next level. You both want to, but don't know quite how to get things going.

AQUARIUS–SCORPIO
KARMA AND VISION

You're both **Fixed** signs who share an instant attraction. But you're so dissimilar, it will take **enormous** effort to stay in the game.

You're both high-maintenance personalities who need special **handling.** His "seasonal theme" is to transform what already exists. Everything he does is motivated by passion, rage, elation, or desire. Scorpios have a fundamental need to prove themselves.

You're a futurist, unburned by earthly concerns. You're scientific. You observe from a distance. At first, you'll try to find a pattern and logic to his behavior without becoming attached.

But, with a Scorpio, it's **impossible** to keep your distance for very long. He pulls you in. And you may not be prepared to hurl yourself into this vortex.

He'll **blindside** you. He's playing out his karma, so expect this relationship to completely **rock your world.** This isn't going to be a day at the beach.

AQUARIUS–SAGITTARIUS
ALMOST PERFECT

The aspect between your Sun signs is conducive to **friendship, partnership,** and more. You create opportunities for each other. You always help one another out.

You respond to his enthusiasm, sweeping ideas, belief in infinite possibilities, and unending quest for knowledge. He loves your honesty and responds to your intelligence.

Basically he's just a real **cool** guy who's up for anything. Romance is his favorite extracurricular activity. And he's good at it. He'll do and say **crazy** things. It's hard to know when he's serious. He knows how to live. Just thinking

AQUARIUS–CAPRICORN
ENTER, ECSTASY

This relationship could start out to be based on a common goal. Like studying together for a major exam, or working together on an important project. You're both Winter signs devoted to the big picture. You may not talk about your **objectives,** but you secretly sense that you could become faithful allies.

So, how do you two self-sufficient individualists break the ice? Very, very slowly.

This is the kind of relationship that could take a very long time to get off the ground. You may be dating other people, or just not attracted romantically at first.

Then, suddenly, overnight, ***wham!*** You see each other for the first time after knowing each other for a year or more. It's like the universe is playing tricks on you.

Even if your lovefest doesn't start like this, your equally independent personalities could make for slow going.

about him gives you goose bumps.

Sagittarians are athletes, explorers, and always looking for their next adventure. To them, every **infatuation** is an opportunity to rack up a new experience. You understand this philosophy, which is why you get along.

Rarely do you do the "cling thing." You're both programmed for independence.

In fact, if there's any area that may need work, it's intimacy. You may both find it easier to be in a crowd than be alone.

MY TAROT CARD
The Magician

IMAGE:

The symbol of infinity hovers over his head. One arm reaches up for guidance. The other points down to the ground, drawing on Mother Nature's gifts. Every tarot suit lies on his worktable.

MEANING:

The Magician uses all of the Tarot's tools—Emotion (Cups), Action (Wands), Thought (Swords), and Money (Pentacles)—to master his environment. The Magician gives the verve to learn, the nerve to create. An Alchemy expert, he also conjures up the fun kind of chemistry.

STAR SIBS

Geena Davis 1-21
Tiffani-Amber Thiessen 1-23
Tatyana Ali 1-24
Bridget Fonda 1-27
Sarah McLaughlin 1-28
Nick Carter 1-28
Elija Wood 1-28
Oprah Winfrey 1-29
Andrew Keegan 1-29
Heather Graham 1-29
Jonny Lang 1-29
Edward Burns 1-29
Christian Bale 1-30

Justin Timberlake 1-31
Minnie Driver 1-31
Jennifer Jason Leigh 2-5
James Spader 2-7
Chris Rock 2-7
Seth Green 2-8
James Dean 2-8
Sheryl Crow 2-11
Jennifer Aniston 2-11
Chynna Phillips 2-12
Judy Blume 2-12
Christina Ricci 2-12
Benicio Del Toro 2-19

COSMIC ADVANTAGES

Communicative

Multitalented

Innovative

Altruistic

Dazzling

Exciting

Organized

Radiant

Artistic

Extraordinary

Original

Skillful

Brainy

Exceptional

Future-oriented

Liberated

Brilliant

Gifted

Luminous

Quick

Standout

Clever

Telepathic

COSMIC CHALLENGES

Witty

Eccentric

Erratic

Aggravated

Jumpy

Edgy

Touchy

Annoyed

Fickle

Anxious

High-strung

Know-it-all

Troubled

Apprehensive

Nervous

Restless

Unpredictable

Discontent

Irregular

Irritable

Tense

Vexed

Distracted

Aquarius

2 6 4

Volatile

Worried

PISCES

FEBRUARY 20 – MARCH 20

COLORS: foamy sea green, fuchsia, khaki, and powder blue

RULING PLANET: neptune

SYMBOL: two fish swimming in opposite directions

SEASON: winter

QUALITY: mutable

ELEMENT: water

BODY: feet, and soles of the feet

FLOWERS: forget-me-not, aster, night-blooming jasmine, and orange blossom

POWER STONES: moonstone, ruby, and tigereye

COUNTRIES: portugal, libya, haiti, and venezuela

VIBRATION: compassionate, hypersensitive, and theatrical

CITIES: rio, warsaw, seville, jerusalem, chicago, and silver spring

ZODIAC HOUSE: twelfth

KEY WORDS: i'm so psychic, my hair hurts!

WHAT AM I LIKE?

SPIRITUAL, SENSITIVE, CHANGEABLE, AND IMAGINATIVE. You're gentle in thought, spirit, and action. You Fish seem to **float** above the clouds, watching stressed-out Earthlings from above.

To put it mildly, you're an escapist. You'll do anything to avoid reality. It could be gossip, other people's predicaments, or an all-consuming infatuation. If it were up to you, you'd **stay in bed** all day, channel surfing, eating junk food, making phone calls, watching romantic movies, or reading mysteries.

Reality is way too harsh for you **Pisces princesses.** The world can be so loud, stressful, and unforgiving, that you wish you could hit the mute button!

You have plenty of outstanding traits, but typically lack the ambition to get things going.

It's not that you're lazy, it's just that

you'd rather fantasize about something than exert all that energy to actually do it. It exhausts you to even think about it!

Your **fantasy** life can seem so real, you may believe you actually did something just by thinking about it. To say you have a tiny little problem distinguishing fantasy from reality is an understatement.

When you *do* find something you like to do, like play guitar, write stories, study acting, and so forth, you can lose track of **time.** You become what you do. You lose yourself in the process and tap into an **inner resource** that can only be described as divine inspiration.

You have plenty of friends. Everyone loves a Pisces! You're accepting, gullible, sympathetic, and always there. Let's face facts: most people are judgmental, opinionated, and need to control things.

Not you. You're not demanding. It's not that you deprive yourself, it's just that you're accepting of others. Inexplicably, around you, people change their tune and relax.

You're the **"warm fuzzy"** kind of friend. When somebody tells you their problems, you could almost swear it's happening to you. You're open to suggestions.

You're always game for some crazy scheme. You don't take too much seriously, and you love to fool around. It's not that you're a rebel, it's just that you don't pay attention to the rules. You usually get away with murder because people buy your **innocent** act.

You find routine mind-numbing. You'll do anything to change the way you feel. You're famous for your stories, excuses, explanations, and little white lies. You love to make things more interesting.

You're drawn to the occult, music, the arts, or anything that alters the way you think. Make-believe is your favorite state of mind.

To a Pisces, reality truly bites.

MY ASTRO HOUSE

TWELVE IS A MYSTICAL NUMBER.

There were twelve apostles, there are **twelve** steps to a spiritual awakening in recovery, and twelve is the official age that ends your **childhood** and the grade that ends your high-school education.

The twelfth house is the last stop in the zodiac. It symbolizes the invisible world, the other side. It deals with the subconscious, prophecy, dreams, hidden motives, psychology, self-destructive behaviors, religion, prayer, and charity.

It also concerns itself with **"confined"** places such as jails, hospitals, institutions, and treatment centers.

It protects and presides over people who devote their lives to these areas. Nurses, prison workers, doctors, psychics, healers, religious personnel, psychiatrists, therapists, and philanthropists.

Hidden forces feel real. You could fall into self-destructive behaviors more rapidly than most. The saving grace of the twelfth house is divine intervention. Your guardian angels won't let you down. **Promise!**

HOW DOES MY PLANETARY RULER, NEPTUNE, AFFECT ME?

Act 1 Scene 1

NEPTUNE IS THE GOD OF THE OCEANS.

It creates **imaginative** thought, dream life, and make-believe. It deceives and deludes. It's what makes love blind. Neptune's power prevents you from seeing people as they are. It **colors** your emotions. It's why you glamorize and romanticize. It distorts reality and makes you believe what you see.

Neptune is the Great Deceiver. It creates impressions and atmosphere. Makeup, fashion, whimsical architecture, glamorous restaurants, the theater world, and even theme parks all fall under Neptune's spell.

Neptune is the higher octave of Venus. Venus is the goddess of romance, beauty, and grace. Neptune elevates these things to the level of glamor. It is myth, folklore, fairy tale, and legend. It is Mount Olympus. It is celebrity and fame. Neptune rules celluloid, the film business, and illusion.

Anything that **propels** you into a different reality is the domain of Neptune.

MY FAMILY

IN YOUR SOLAR HORO-SCOPE, witty, busy Gemini influences the domestic fourth house and sets the tone at home.

Your house could feel like **a bee-hive.** Everybody talks at once. You have more relatives than you can count. Multiple marriages and visitors are likely. Your parents could emphasize reading, writing, and advanced education. **Grades** take on tremendous importance. No one is allowed to slack off.

Education is a priority. Reading is your link to the world. Frequent travel and excursions could be a family tradition.

Your parents could be young at heart, **lively,** and have unbelievably exciting jobs. Or they could be incredibly irresponsible and you could find yourself having to supervise yourself. You may even feel that the burden of keeping the family going is somehow your responsibility.

Your siblings could be your closest friends in the world. Or if things are out of alignment, you could be estranged from a brother or sister for a very long time due to circumstances beyond your control.

WHAT SHOULD I BE DOING

YOU'RE AN ESCAPIST. You see the world through **rose-colored** glasses and will probably find a place in the world that requires imagination. You'll try to find a place in society that encourages you to stay connected to your dream world. Like teaching children, writing books, or working on movies.

You are quick on the uptake, but could fall into **space-cadet**

CAREER

YOU'RE PHILOSOPHICAL WHEN IT COMES TO WORK AND CAREER. You don't believe in wasting your life on something meaningless. You need to find something **meaningful** that makes a difference in the world.

That's why **parenthood** appeals to most Pisces. The idea of creating a new life is the ultimate experience that defies explanation. You could **devote** your life to teaching kids, working with kids in other respects, or studying child development.

Many Fish work as actors, comedians, dancers, figure skaters, singers, and writers. You **excel** in any field designed to enhance reality or depart from it.

Basically, whatever job doesn't feel like a job is the thing you want to do.

WITH MY LIFE?

syndrome if you don't **focus** and let your mind wander.

Pay attention to your **hunches, dreams,** and intuitions. For a Pisces, these things could actually be a signal from your unconscious.

If you have the dream, then you have the **power** to make it real.

STAR TIPS ON FASHION, HEALTH, AND BEAUTY

NEPTUNE, MASTER OF ILLUSION, RULES YOUR SIGN. This comes in handy with the blush brush, your **makeup paint** box, and a little sleight of hand. You leave your friends breathless when they see how you deftly transform from schoolgirl to party girl as if the old you has disappeared.

With **colors,** try to reflect the ocean with Mediterranean blue, aqua, coral reef, and water-lily white.

With your clothes, **know** your body type! You're happiest when you're comfortable. Capri pants or leggings and a basic T-shirt suit you just fine.

Pisces rules the feet, so build up your shoe collection. Adorn the feet with sexy toe rings. Pamper those piggies with pedicures and fab nail colors.

The sole of your foot has acupuncture points that stimulate every major organ and muscle group in your body. Foot rubs will maintain your balance and send you into outer space!

You're probably a swimmer. Use two-in-one shampoo-plus-conditioner to save time. Minimize blow-drying: the heat depletes natural oils. Experiment with tints and colors that wash out easily. Barrettes, wide-toothed clips, and elastics prevent a meltdown on a bad-hair day.

With skin care and makeup, less is more. Goes-on-creamy, stays-on-dry foundations work well.

Have sunblock with SPF 30 handy when you fry in the sun. You Pisces love the tub, so stock up on sea-based body potions, spa scrubs, mineral salts, and rain forest bath gels.

CUSP KIDZ

AQUARIUS–PISCES: FEBRUARY 18–22

Since the oncoming Sun sign power always overtakes the outgoing power of the previous sign, if you're born on this cusp you're primarily Pisces with a pinch of Aquarius. Aquarius prevents you from completely losing yourself in your famous Neptunian dreamscape. This is the **Cusp of Inspiration.** Aquarian originality nurtures the Pisces imagination. You're a **double threat!**

Your solar strengths of compassion, empathy, creativity, and psychic ability are maxed out, girl! Add to this the genius, telepathy, and individual qualities attributed to Aquarius and you've got a **can't-fail** combo! Cha-cha-cha!

PISCES–ARIES: MARCH 18–22

Talk about doing the cha-cha-cha! This is the **Cusp of Invincibility.** What a blend!

With upcoming Aries, you are a special brand of emotion and fire. With the outgoing influence of Pisces, sure, you know things before they happen but you are never quite, or exactly, sure when this otherworldly information is going to enter your **subconscious.**

You only hope that this time it will pertain to things that are important to you. Why, oh why, you ask yourself so many times, does the **psychic** info have absolutely nothing to do with you?

This feeling is **doubled,** even **tripled,** because you are *so* on the edge of the "me" sign of Aries.

COSMIC LOVE MATCHES

PISCES–PISCES
MARINE DREAMS

It's like when you don't **water** a plant you stare at every day. You know it needs water, but **inertia** washes over you and you watch it dry up and die. It's not a deliberate thing, you're just indifferent.

When this relationship **loses steam,** check for a pulse.

Two Pisces together can be an impossible dream unless your charts have a powerful ascendant, moon, or other **energetic** planetary placements.

You bring out the dreamer in each other. Even if you both promise to do better, work harder, set goals, or just get in the car and go to the mall, you usually wind up letting **time** slip away and then you think, Why bother?

On a more **optimistic** note, this can be a **sensual** and loving connection. You both lean toward the arts, and you'd make a **terrific** writing or musical team. Your imaginations run wild when you're together. You can be sympathetic partners who feel inexplicably linked by a force greater than yourselves.

Why fight fate?

Astro Glitch

Even though this can be a really relaxed, enjoyable, and emotionally satisfying love match, you're both so passive that it could die from neglect. It's not that you don't want it to work, it's just that you're lazy.

PISCES–ARIES
FANTASY VERSUS REALITY

You're an **evolved** Winter sign who straddles this world and the other. He's a **reckless** spring spirit who lives in and for the moment. Even if the **"other side"** exists, he doesn't have time to deal with what he can't see. He might not admit it, but he's **amazed** at your ability to feel. He can't understand your depth or sensitivity.

PISCES—TAURUS
NOURISH AND FLOURISH

This love match can go a long way. You fit together like an Oreo cookie and are just as delicious! Your Sun signs form an auspicious aspect that leads to good fortune. Your elements, Earth and **Water,** mix well.

His unwavering and dependable character helps bring you down from the clouds. But by the same token, you remind him that there's more to life than meets the eye. You trigger his **imagination** and inspire him to test his limits.

Your Bull just won't let go, which can feel unbelievably flattering.

His good traits surpass his bad ones. He's good with money and takes care of business. He loves to **indulge** himself by living the good life and will spoil you, too. It's hard for him to express himself in words, he'd rather say it with flowers, CDs and other goodies.

His stubborn side is obvious. He derives pleasure from having a **routine** and playing it safe. He's not exactly the most spontaneous guy in the world. But the upside of this is that he'll stick around longer than you expect.

Astro Glitch

Your Taurus is possessive. You're a free spirit who doesn't believe you can own other people. His jealousy can disturb you. You honestly don't know how to handle that kind of stuff.

He thinks it's great you're like that, but he can't be **bothered** with such things.

You're impressed with his energy, but his blatant insensitivity scares you off. He doesn't care what people think. He's to die for.

When he zeros in on you for the kill, you're toast. He has that kind of **charisma.** You can take him in small doses, but you may ultimately get in over your head. Once you're involved, you give and **give** and give.

Your faith in people can keep you in limbo, waiting for him to change, long after he's left the scene. Protect yourself. As fast as he came into your life is as fast as he can **split.**

Astro Alert

Rams have a notoriously short attention span. They're mouth-watering but emotionally challenged. He's just not as complicated as you give him credit for. He simply lacks the capacity to give as much as you. You have completely different systems of measurement.

Pisces
275

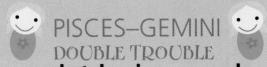

PISCES–GEMINI
DOUBLE TROUBLE

This relationship can be an **intriguing puzzle** due to your equally dual personalities.

He's the Twin with two distinct personalities. He can be all things to all people. You're never sure who you're getting. He can switch during the course of a single conversation. Your astrological symbol depicts two fish swimming in opposite directions. This illustrates your tendency to get **confused,** be of two minds, or be in two worlds simultaneously.

This may not be the most stable coupling, but it certainly holds your interest and keeps you on your toes. You never know what to expect. His feelings for you are a mystery. Even though he'll flake, bail, and disappoint, you're incapable of staying angry because he's just so **adorable.**

You're changeable, moody, and impressionable. Your feelings for him can flip-flop overnight. His frenzied energy only makes things more volatile.

Astro Hint

Our fleet-footed Gemini is flirtatious, fun, and always seems to have something going on. He's plugged in to everything. Unfortunately, many things don't include you. Sure, he's great when he's around, but you need to decide if he's worth the exasperation.

PISCES–CANCER
SOFTSHELL CRAB

This **Water trine** can creep up on you like a tidal wave and have as big of an effect. Neither of you is prepared for the volcanic emotions that wash over you. This coupling could turn into the biggest love of your life.

But don't get carried away just yet. . . .

Unlike most signs who can be easily controlled and manipulated by a Cancer, you have this amazing ability to **wrap** him around your little finger.

When a Cancer loves something or somebody, they'll do anything to **protect** their interest. He'll be attentive, romantic,

PISCES–LEO
A SOLO PERFORMANCE

Unless there are **significant** modifying factors, this combo can have a relatively **short** life span. The Lion may be too much for the Fish.

The male Leo is a **force** to be reckoned with. He's a modern soldier, always engaged in some **dramatic** controversy, power play, or battle. He may not be fighting for anything more important than an allowance boost.

The Leo is a **strong, generous, and regal** creature who acts like he owns the world. This couldn't be further from who you are. You don't even care about this world as much as you do preparing for the next!

He's a **born actor.** He needs to find a role to express himself. This explains why he is such a Romeo. His performance can completely fool you.

He loves the sound of his voice. He's convinced he's always right. He barely lets you **get a word in** edgewise, and you're so spun out that you forget what you were going to say.

Astro Alert

Ultimately, he could be too exhausting a project for you to take on. His constant need for attention gets old real fast. There just doesn't seem to be room enough for both of you.

and on his best behavior. He'll try to curb those titanic moods and not be so cranky.

He's the kind of boyfriend who calls every day. Who plans stuff on the weekends. Who takes pictures to preserve the **memories.**

No matter what side he presents to the world, you're the only one who gets to see the dark side of the moon.

Astro Hint

You know he needs security and nurturing whether or not he tells you, and this you can provide. He becomes a devoted puppy around you.

PISCES–VIRGO
SENSE AND SENSIBILITY

Have you finally met your solar **opposite?** If you don't drive each other nuts with your glaring differences, this could be one of the most rewarding relationships possible.

You two can make a **terrific team** if you learn to be accepting, open-minded, and willing to compromise. A Virgo can streamline your life and give you focus. It's not that you don't have it, it's just that you're not sure what it is.

For instance, let's say you're a musical prodigy. You may not even know it, but you just love to play music. A Virgo will see your talent as a **means to an end.** He'll show you how to put things in a **practical** framework.

Same thing with romance. You may be happy drifting along with no particular goals. But if his **feelings** are strong for you, you can bet he'll do something about it to make sure it's heading in the right direction.

He gives you **form.** You give him permission to be emotional. Virgo lives by logic and reason, but matters of the heart **defy** explanation. You can guide him through this unchartered territory.

Astro Fact

You're sloppy, he's neat. You take things as they come. He's mapped out his future. You don't worry about things that haven't occurred. He's already stressing about what's going to happen in five years.

PISCES–LIBRA
THE LANGUAGE OF LOVE

This love link can be a dream come true. Neptune is the higher octave of Venus, so you're both **die-hard romantics.**

Together, you tune out the world. Nobody else matters.

With you, he just might get **hooked.** You have this terminally feminine vibration that makes him crazy.

You love the **escapist** aspect to this bond. You go with the flow. You throw yourself into this relationship with complete abandon.

The only **glitch** is that his "progress report" mentality might get on your nerves. He likes to take **stock** of

PISCES–SCORPIO
RAW EMOTION

People underestimate you. Your looks deceive. You appear fragile and easy to break. Not so. Never is your strength so apparent when confronted with the mighty Scorpio.

Your suns form the gratifying trine aspect, suggesting compatibility and understanding.

As the last Water sign, you're the most evolved and he knows it. What's really cool is that you don't feel the need to prove yourself like he does and it kind of blows his mind. You make him see how ridiculous his struggles, judgments, and opinions really are. Next to him, you seem practically conflict-free.

This could be an intense and passionate experience for the both of you. When he gets grabby, angry, or tries to control things, you'd rather flee than fight. This throws him for a loop. It also makes him reflect on his behavior.

where you're at and talk about your relationship as if it's a college course. For you, this dissection defeats the purpose of falling in love. It's supposed to defy logic.

Because of your mutual need to bond, you may agree to become exclusive relatively fast. You don't see any reason not to.

Astro Alert

When the "we" sign enters your life, prepare to embark on an adventure of the heart. He's serious about dating. He's engrossed in making it work. To him, it's a competitive sport. And he's usually triumphant.

Astro Insight

This astro match creates profound emotion and sensuality. Together, you will go through many phases of growth. The Scorpio lets his guard down around you. He stops fighting and being so defensive. He shows you his vulnerable side: the scared little boy inside who doesn't know it all. He feels safe with you.

PISCES–SAGITTARIUS
SPONTANEOUS COMBUSTION

Mr. Spiritual meets **Miss Mystical** on campus. You are his latest fascination and will play a recurring role in the movie of your life. Prepare to be **unprepared** with his peekaboo antics. You know, here today, gone tomorrow.

Not that you're a **realist,** but you automatically know not to get your expectations up with him. You're content to hang out with him when he's around because he's such a character. His **enthusiasm** gets your heart started. The world seems more exciting when you're around him.

He's the type to **sweep** you off your feet with grand gestures and **shock** you into doing things you wouldn't do with anyone else. Like pull out your mountain bike, ice skates, hiking boots, sailing gear, snow skis, or anything involved with fun, sports, and adventures. His bouts of **wanderlust** don't bother you. It takes you enough time to recover between episodes. But you'll drop everything when he suddenly arrives and never fails to turn your world upside down.

Astro Alert

If he's a "bad boy," he'll rope you into playing hooky, blowing curfew, and taking risks. He never worries about the consequence of his actions. That's not his style. It's pure adrenaline around him. Be careful!

PISCES–CAPRICORN
BOOKENDS

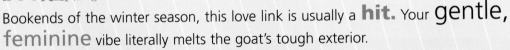

Bookends of the winter season, this love link is usually a **hit.** Your **gentle, feminine** vibe literally melts the goat's tough exterior.

You could be slamming the soccer ball in the goal, sweat pouring down your face, and he'll *still* think that you're the **sweetest** thing in the world.

This coupling is found frequently in marriages. His goal-oriented philosophy

PISCES–AQUARIUS
BRAINTEASER

The Aquarian guy could **change your life.** One day you're minding your own business, and the next, he's transferred into your school, spots you, and that's that. Other girls may try to get his attention and make obvious plays for his affection, but he's attracted to the fact that you are practically oblivious.

Once he gets your attention, it's a matter of minutes before you get completely hooked. The physical attraction is usually strong, but you could find it very frustrating to get close to him.

You need intimacy—it's like oxygen. He doesn't operate that way. He comes off almost cold, certainly indifferent. It's strange, but that's the way he is. He's scientific, logical, and exists in the world of ideas, not emotion.

Just when you think he'll always be distant, he'll blurt out how strongly he feels about you. This **stumps** you even more because what he says and what he does seem to have no connection at all.

He's a walking **brainteaser.** Ultimately, you'll probably realize you need somebody less nerve-racking.

helps you focus. He inspires you to go after what you want in a systematic way.

A Capricorn guy can relax and be himself around you. You don't make him feel like he needs to prove himself. He finds you easy to be with. He loves your **wacky** perceptions. You rely on his common sense. You make him stop beating up on himself so much. He brings clarity where there was only confusion.

MY TAROT CARD
The Empress

IMAGE:

She sits on her velvet throne. Venus's symbol is etched into a heart shaped stone at her feet. The rare pomegranate fruit decorates her flowing robe. Crowned with a star-encrusted tiara, she holds a magic wand with confidence.

MEANING:

The Empress nurtures. Unconditionally, she gives love, therefore she attracts love. She embraces her body and soul. The Empress encourages you to befriend tangled emotions and trust intuition. The universe endows Empress energy with fertility and magnetism.

STAR SIBS

Brian Littrell 2-20
Kurt Cobain 2-20
Lili Taylor 2-20
Cindy Crawford 2-20
Jennifer Love Hewitt 2-21
Drew Barrymore 2-22
Kristin Davis 2-24
Billy Zane 2-24
Téa Leoni 2-25
Sean Astin 2-25
Chelsea Clinton 2-27
Elizabeth Taylor 2-27
Robert Sean Leonard 2-28
Antonio Sabato, Jr. 2-29
Mark-Paul Gosselaar 3-1
Dr. Seuss 3-2
Jon Bon Jovi 3-2
Jackie Joyner-Kersee 3-3
Jessica Biel 3-3
Shaquille O'Neal 3-6

Rachel Weisz 3-7
James Van Der Beek 3-8
Freddie Prinze Jr. 3-8
Juliette Binoche 3-9
Sharon Stone 3-10
Jasmine Guy 3-10
Thora Birch 3-11
Lisa Loeb 3-11
Jordan Taylor Hanson 3-14
Billy Crystal 3-14
Albert Einstein 3-14
Todd McFarlane 3-16
Billy Corgan 3-17
Mia Hamm 3-17
Rob Lowe 3-17
Queen Latifah 3-18
Vanessa Williams 3-18
Bruce Willis 3-19
Glenn Close 3-19
Michael Rapaport 3-20

COSMIC ADVANTAGES

Compassionate

Inspired

Psychic

Artistic

Dedicated

Hip

Intuitive

Attentive

Devoted

Magical

Otherworldly

Authentic

Dutiful

Imaginative

Spiritual

Caring

Faithful

Individualistic

Mystical

Swoon-worthy

Clairvoyant

Quick

COSMIC CHALLENGES

Thoughtful

Absentminded

Fly-by-night

Forgetful

Changeable

Hazy

Scatterbrained

Confused

Unclear

Hermit

Depressive

Indecisive

Undependable

Unreliable

Doubtful

Lazy

Nebulous

Unsure

Escapist

Slacker

Vague

Pisces
2 8 4

ASTROLOGY JOURNAL

DEBRA LEVERE is an astrology expert who has written the astrology columns for several major magazines, including *Jump*, *Detour*, and *L.A. Weekly*. She has also done private readings for numerous mega-celebrities. A Capricorn, she lives in Los Angeles, California.

MONICA GESUE's irresistible artwork can be found in most of the leading teen magazines. This talented Taurus lives in Connecticut.